BEYOND THE DARK N

BEYOND
THE DARK NIGHT

A Way Forward for the Church?

MARY C. GREY

CASSELL

Cassell
Wellington House, 125 Strand, London WC2R 0BB
PO Box 605, Herndon, VA 20172

First published 1997

British Library Cataloguing-in-Publication Data
A catalogue record for this book is available from the British Library.

ISBN 0-304-33753-6

Typeset by York House Typographic Ltd, London
Printed and bound in Great Britain by
Biddles Ltd, Guildford and King's Lynn

CONTENTS

ACKNOWLEDGEMENTS

We are grateful for permission to reproduce the following:

(p. 7) extract from Emilie Townes, *A Troubling in My Soul*, by permission of Orbis Books;

(p. 67) Mary Oliver, 'Peonies' from *New and Selected Poems*, published by Beacon Press;

(p. 102) extract from Toni Morrison, *Beloved*, by permission of International Creative Management, Inc.;

see pp. 104–5 for Carter Heyward, 'Blessing the Bread: a Litany';

(p. 112) prayer from *Confessing Our Faith Around the World*, vol. 4, by permission of the World Council of Churches;

(p. 127) extract from Euripides, *Medea*, translated by Rex Warner, by permission of David Higham Associates.

(p. 142) May Sarton, 'A Grain of Mustard Seed' from *Journal of a Solitude*, published in Great Britain by The Women's Press Ltd, 34 Great Sutton Street, London EC1V 0DX, used by permission of The Women's Press Ltd.

PREFACE

No, not another book on the Church! I hear the groans ... Why try again to argue that in this multi-cultural, multi-faith, postmodern society the Church has a valuable role? Surely the disillusioned have already gone, while for those who stay it is not even a question? As I write, the significance of two events rings in my ears. The first is the grief felt by thousands of Christians – far beyond the Roman Catholic Church – at the excommunication of the Sri Lankan liberation theologian Tissa Balasuriya, the Oblate of Mary Immaculate.[1] That he, aged 72, a life-long fighter for the poor, who in 1979 opened up the whole question of the heart of the Eucharist being for the poor, the broken-hearted and dispossessed, should now be excluded from Christ's communion table![2]

The second event was the recent joyful declaration[3] of a coalition of many radical groups of Roman Catholics, the Jubilee People coalition, that 'We are Church'. It was an attempt to take with absolute seriousness the intuition of the Second Vatican Council that the pilgrim people of God, the baptized community of faithful, do constitute the pulsating heart of the community of discipleship. That this affirmation could happen against the background of the tragic excommunication suggests that there is a *wellspring of hope* that prophetic Church can still rise from the ashes of despair, from what I am calling throughout this book the *Dark Night of the Church*.

There is still another reason for this book. For many years I – along with many parents and friends – have watched in anguish the steady disillusionment of our children with the Church. We have seen them grow from bored but obedient children to rebellious and disenchanted teenagers, who found that their concerns for peace, ecology, justice and meaningful participation were better met outside than in the Church. Many of them are themselves wounded by abuse from the very priests whom they trusted and saw as Christ's representatives. Yet they have usually looked in vain for understanding and pastoral sensitivity with regard to the pattern of their own sexual relationships; and in vain for forgiveness and welcome when their marriages failed and they still wanted to belong.

Yet these are the same young people who could cry – with other groups – on 7 December 'We are Church' ... And this cry has sprung forth at the same moment as the Roman Catholic bishops have published a significant document, *The Common Good*,[4] which, whatever its flaws and omissions,[5] makes a powerful plea that social justice issues should be seen as clear priorities during the British election campaign in 1997 – and beyond. Again this is part of the same *wellspring of hope* – and it is this which is the inspiration for the picture on the front of this book. It is a photograph taken by my husband, Nicholas, in one of our journeys to the desert of Rajasthan, as part of the work of Wells for India.[6] It is in fact the sunlight hitting the bottom of the well, where there is still a little water. We have used it as a symbol of the way water brings new life and new hope to the people of the desert. I use it here to symbolize the wellspring of hope which is the *rising of prophetic Church* from the ashes of despair, alienation and the corruption of power. And I dedicate this book to my family, my friends and colleagues – to all of you who wait in the *Dark Night* – with the hope that the Morning Star is on the horizon, and that we may yet, like Simeon of old, behold her rising.

Notes

1 I have alluded to the possibility of this excommunication throughout the book. The final decision was only reported in *The Tablet* (11 January 1997), p. 50 (Vatican text, p. 51).

2 See Tissa Balasuriya, *The Eucharist and Human Liberation* (London: SCM, 1979).

3 On 7 December 1996.

4 The Catholic Bishops' Conference of England and Wales, *The Common Good* (Manchester: Gabriel Communications, 1996).

5 One glaring omission is that this document is almost totally *gender-blind*.

6 Wells for India was founded in 1987 by Nicholas Grey, Ramsahai Purohit and myself. Originally focusing on building wells, we have moved to water-harvesting, medical, social and educational work.

INTRODUCTION: BEYOND THE DARK NIGHT

The Word blew its spirit over the dried bones of the churches, guardians of silence.[1]

Guardians of silence, or *guardians of the silenced?* Is this how we experience the reality of the Churches today? It would certainly seem so from the media point of view! As yet one more theologian is compelled to silence, as yet another case of cover-up of child abuse by the clergy is revealed, one more corruption scandal, another woman discriminated against, another person refused the sacraments – and this is merely to mention a few stumbling blocks – the despair of many Christians whose faith is deeply rooted in Scripture and the living out of faith according to Gospel values grows daily. Silence comes to be experienced not as the wordless contemplation of the sacred mystery, but as the numbed reaction to alienation, exclusion from power and authority, loss of inspirational leadership and the disempowerment of blind obedience. That *the Church is alive with trivialities and oppressive legalism* is a frequent accusation. There is a danger that we become the sheep of the flock all too literally, if, as it sometimes seems, the only authorized response is passive infantilism. In a moment of despair, it could even be said that, in a frightening reversal, unlike Nero, who fiddled while Rome burnt, *Rome is in danger of fiddling while the planet is destroyed and hunger for justice is anaesthetized by contemporary versions of bread and circuses and transformed into violence.*

Is it true, then, that the Churches are simply *dinosaurs of irrelevance* in a secular world? Are their liturgies merely *shrines of boredom* for the vast majority? As vast numbers of young people leave the Church, and second and third generations of young people grow up out of touch with their spiritual ancestry,[2] as is happening now in most countries of Western Europe; and as increasing numbers of women, gay communities and ethnic minorities recount their stories of painful discrimination and exclusion, must this be the dismal conclusion?[3] And if so, what integrity is there for those within the assumed 'categories of respectability' hanging on to Church membership? Surely solidarity with marginal people demands a dignified exit, a search for a wider notion of justice, and an attempt to build the *truly human* with our fellow secularized citizens?[4]

This book is written with the conviction that we are at the moment experiencing the *Dark Night of the Church*. And yet it is written with a deeply rooted love of the Church. Although I write as a lifelong committed Roman Catholic, I now write deliberately in an ecumenical way, exploring how the very notion of Church can be made more accessible and the Church itself be once again experienced as a place for healing, reconciliation and liberation. Although this book will at times be sharply critical, the aim is to move beyond the divisive polarities of left/right, traditional/progressive, and to be receptive to fresh insights as to the meaning of Christian discipleship in community. Although it will seem to privilege the wisdom which comes from below, it is not denying the need for structure and good governance: rather, it seeks out a different voice, hoping that the 'voices crying in the wilderness' may be heard by the Church, recalling her to the prophetic witness of the crucified peoples of today.

Time and again I see the Church failing a generation of young people. Recently, when teaching a course on 'The Church' at the Catholic University of Nijmegen, in The Netherlands, together with the students I had spent the whole week discerning significant dimensions of Christian life which would enable liberation, truth, justice for creation, transformation of society, wholeness of humanity and so on. When I set them the task of imagining a Church where all of this could be realized, I was astonished and grieved by the violence of their reaction. *This was just not possible.* They were not prepared even to waste time thinking about it! Any journey of liberation would be sought outside the Church structures – but I suspect that it would not be sought at all. Rather, their theology would run the risk of being once again a theoretic exercise, divorced from lived experience. I have encountered a similar level of estrangement in many countries in Western and Central Europe.

Truly, the *Dark Night of the Church*. But is the only answer an exodus from the Church, as Mary Daly made on a famous occasion at Harvard University, calling women to follow her?[5] Does the cry of Peter, 'Lord, to whom shall we go?', still ring across the centuries to those who, despite the odds, still yearn after 'the words of eternal life' (John 6:68)? Is this cultural despair a phenomenon confined merely to Western Europe? Indeed, in many other parts of the world, the contrary is happening: women are rediscovering biblical stories as stories of liberating justice.[6] In fact, the Women-Church movement is now a global movement of women and men seeking and expressing a Church which affirms the full humanity of women and is committed to eradicating the many interlocking oppressions from which humans and non-humans suffer.[7] Nor is the Women-Church movement alone in struggling to burgeon forth new expressions of Church. It would be difficult to identify a period when there were so many prophetic (albeit somewhat marginal) and ecumenical (sometimes interfaith) groups, such as Justice and Peace groups, ecological spirituality groups, the Open Synod Group (Church of England), Catholics for a Changing Church (Roman Catholic), Femmes et Hommes dans L'Église (Paris), Christians in Public Life programmes, the justice spiritualities of the Aid Agencies, the Iona Community, Taizé, and so on. Is this a phenomenon which could offset the gloom of the criticism with which I began?

The efforts of all such groups give me confidence to use the metaphor of the Dark Night in a double way. There is a danger that to speak metaphorically will be seen as weakening the realities I describe. Yet nothing can detract from the fact that the alienation and despair, the painful experience of receiving injustice from a source that one could justifiably expect to be nourishing, a nourishing source of community, strikes at the core of one's being. 'I gave my life, my soul to the Church and look what has happened . . .' is the anguished cry of many voices, both male and female. It is the unvoiced cry of those whose grief is too inchoate, inarticulate, choked at the roots, whose voices have been stilled by the 'guardians of the silenced'. It is the Dark Night of the Church where God's Spirit seems absent, where the dreaded question has to be faced: is Christ still with his Church? So I use the metaphor of the 'Dark Night' intentionally playing on its double meaning. In the current struggle against racism it is important to recover the many positive means of darkness and blackness. Darkness is also a metaphor for the hiddenness and mystery of God.

It is the strength of Christian feminist mysticism which insists that the Dark Night experience is an embodied experience and must stay close to the reality of fear and violence which the Dark Night means for women and girls; which insists on grounding the spiritual experience of Dark Night in the practical goal of 'Take back the Night!'[8] Make the streets safe for young girls to walk without fear, for children not to be assaulted or given drugs.

But the Dark Night of the mystics carries another significance.[9] It is the sense that the absence is a pregnant one. That something new is being formed. That a new dawn is being ushered in. But it may be that this new baby, this new way of being Church, is not yet fully formed and ready. The ancient Jewish stance of waiting on the Lord, hoping, longing, may be what is required in this Dark Night, as we await a mystical breakthrough:

I wait for the Lord, my soul waits,
and in his word I hope;
my soul waits for the Lord
more than watchmen for the morning . . .
O Israel, hope in the Lord!
For with the Lord there is steadfast love,
and with him is plentiful redemption.

(Psalm 130:5–6, 7)

Not that this means a passive stance. Or even a 'washing of our hands', Pontius Pilate-like, of the structures and movements which work for this breakthrough. For us not to use the insights and efforts which have arisen in our times could be to ignore the very structures of grace which the Holy Spirit is offering.

The aim of this book is to weave together these epiphanies of grace[10] – glimpsed in the ecumenical and interfaith movements, the many struggles for justice, peace, for the ordination of women, for the integrity of creation and in the more secular hunger for justice and for spirituality – into a theology of Church which responds to the pain of the Dark Night. But the hope is that it will bring us *beyond the Dark Night*, into a new experience of being a Christian community towards the millennium. As such, it will be neither one-sidedly prophetic nor narrowly mystical, but exploring both dimensions. It will be feminist, ecumenical, liberationist, and will draw on the richness of the Christian tradition – and, where appropriate, on other faiths. It will build on the relational theology of my two earlier works, *Redeeming the Dream* and *The Wisdom of Fools?*, seeking to weave the passion for justice which drove the former, and the radical questioning as to the channels of God's communication which drove the latter, into an ecclesiology for today. An ecclesiology for a pilgrim people, still following the star, seeking, like the sparrow in Bede's story, a little light, a little warmth and love – and an immense amount of justice. But most of all, *seeking God.*[11]

Notes

1 Julia Esquivel, *Threatened with Resurrection* (Elgin, IL: The Brethren Press, 1982), cited in *Bread of Tomorrow*, ed. Janet Morley (London: Christian Aid and SPCK, 1993), p. 47.

2 William K. Kay, Leslie J. Francis (eds), *Drift from the Churches* (Cardiff: University of Wales Press, 1996).

3 See Dorothea McEwan (ed.), *Women Experiencing Church* (Leominster: Gracewing, 1992); Margaret Hart, *To Have a Voice: Network of Ecumenical Women in Scotland* (Edinburgh: St Andrew's Press, 1995); Rosie Miles, *Not in Our Name: Voices of Women Who Have Left the Church* (Nottingham: Southwell Diocese Social Responsibility Group, 1994).

4 In no way am I ignoring Britain's multi-cultural realities. There is not a choice between Christianity or secularism and never has been. Indeed, one of the purposes of this book is to argue for a theology of Church based on interfaith dialogue. But I am facing the fact of the 'establishment' of the Church of England, which not only does not reflect the true situation, but overshadows the diversity of faith communities which flourish. Indeed, secularism has infected the very heart of all our faith realities.

5 See Daphne Hampson, 'Exodus or not?' in *Yearbook of the European Society of Women in Theological Research* III (August 1995) (Mainz: Grünewald and Kampen: Kok), pp. 73–83.

6 See, for example, Rigoberta Menchú, 'The Bible and self-defense' in *Feminist Theology from the Third World*, ed. Ursula King (London: SPCK and Maryknoll: Orbis, 1994), pp. 183–8, as well as other contributions to this volume.

7 The literature on Women-Church is growing. I attempted to summarize its origins and its significance in M. Grey, *The Wisdom of Fools?* (London: SPCK, 1993), ch. 9, 'The Church: permanently marginal or leaven for change?', pp. 120–36.

8 I have developed this point in M. Grey, *Redeeming the Dream* (London: SPCK, 1989), p. 75.

9 See John of the Cross, *The Dark Night* in *John of the Cross: Selected Writings*, ed. Kieran Kavanaugh (London: SPCK, 1987); Oliver Davies, *Meister Eckhart: Mystical Theologian* (London: SPCK, 1991).

10 I coined this phrase in *The Wisdom of Fools?*, pp. 60–1. For me it encapsulates the way the Spirit can find cracks in the culture and create openings for new life, grace and justice. 'Epiphany' stresses that this moment is given and revealed through the ordinary processes of life.

11 'Your majesty, when we compare the present life of man on earth with that time of which we have no knowledge, it seems to me like the swift flight of a single sparrow through the banqueting-hall, when you are sitting at dinner with your thanes and counsellors. In the midst, there is a comforting fire to warm the Hall; outside, the storms of winter rain or snow are raging. This sparrow flies swiftly in through one door of the Hall, and out through another. While he is inside, he is safe from the winter storms; but after a few moments of comfort, he vanishes from sight into the wintry world from which he came. Even so, man appears on earth for a little while; but of what went before this life, or what follows, we know nothing': Bede, *A History of the English Church and People*, trans. and intro. Leo Sherley-Price (Harmondsworth: Penguin, 1955), ch. 13, p. 127.

PART ONE

SEARCHING FOR SOUL IN CONTEMPORARY SOCIETY

I believe the soul is that part of man that he is least aware of, particularly the West European, for I think that orientals 'live' their soul more fully. We Westerners don't know what to do with them; indeed we are ashamed of our souls as if they were something immoral. 'Soul' is very different from what we call 'heart'. There are plenty of people who have a lot of 'heart' but very little 'soul'.
(Etty Hillesum, *An Interrupted Life: The Diaries of Etty Hillesum 1941–3* (New York: Washington Square Press, 1985), pp. 240–1)

Evil is a force outside us
suffering makes you stronger
lies
lies
lies
to my very deepest soul
there is a troubling in my soul.
(Emilie M. Townes (ed.), *A Troubling in My Soul: Womanist Perspectives on Evil and Suffering* (Maryknoll: Orbis, 1993), introductory quotation)

I

SEARCHING FOR SOUL

To ask new questions about the significance of being Church today presumes another level of understanding the world we live in. It presumes we have a handle on this world, that we can accurately describe it, and know its needs and yearnings most intimately. No one believes the Church survives, triumphalist and smug, without any consciousness of responding to the human situation. The developments of the last 40 years, since the founding of the World Council of Churches in 1948 in Amsterdam, have shown that this enormously diverse group of global Christian communities has made impressive efforts, not just to bridge the Church–world gap, but to carve out a whole new relationship with the world in some areas. Yet, not only the Church's failures in other areas, but the shifting sands of culture, and the new political-economic situation, demand that this Church–world relationship be more radically teased out and a new approach discovered. Otherwise, building a new theology of Church would be only to polish the cabin doorknobs on the *Titanic*, or to insist on keeping a finger in the dyke when the ocean is streaming over our heads. Hence these three chapters of Part One explore the context in which a radical rethinking of the contextual positioning of Church takes place. This chapter seeks new metaphors for describing society. Chapter 2 relates these to traditional ways of understanding Church — which it questions — and the third chapter constructs a new beginning as a response to a changing context.

The thread which underlies these chapters is the wish to restore theology to ordinary people of faith. This is neither to surrender to individualism, exaggerated democracy, nor to re-enter the deep tensions between charism and institution. Nor is it to dispute that order, structure and government are necessary, even crucial to a theology of Church. *But it is to put people at the heart of this process.* It is to claim that the activity of theologizing is a deeply meaningful human activity which discloses God's presence within the life of faith, and makes claims on human beings continually, challenging us to explore and celebrate structures of grace — not structures of sin, nor structures which

8

stifle human freedom to grow in harmony with the rhythms of the cosmos.

And, finally, it is a theology which is not divorced from spirituality. Spirituality is viewed here in an immensely practical way as an *enabling discipline, as providing the tools to make life in God's presence a reality, our dreams achievable.* (This will be developed in Chapter 10.) So many of my generation have spent lifetimes of longing for the Church of our dreams to appear. In doing so, in waiting for 'the angel of the Church' to appear with the blueprint for action – as in the Book of Revelation – we have missed out on nourishment; our roots have withered till we cry out with the poet,

> Mine, O thou Lord of life, send my roots rain.[1]

Could this be a *kairos* moment to re-root ourselves in a more profound theological vision and praxis for Christian community, and to rediscover this from the position of marginality? Or from a position which two recent writers, Hannah Ward and Jennifer Wild, described as 'creative boundary living'?[2]

But first, prophetic marginality as a positive stance needs to be seen to flow from an appreciation of a specific reading of culture. Culture is here considered as a kaleidoscope of how we interpret the interwoven strands of politics, economics, technology, as well as all the juridical and aesthetic expressions in art, architecture, music and literature. Culture is expressed by the stories we tell, the myths we live by, the longings which become embedded in stone, text – or shopping malls! Culture is dependent on how the community memory is enshrined in all of these (as will be explored in Chapter 6). It will be crucial to understand what a culture includes and excludes and how the dominant cultural story interrelates with smaller groups in its midst. And the life of faith is seen as a strand weaving in and out of all that goes to form the cultural mix.

A culture in fragments

Nearly fifty years ago it was *not* the metaphor of fragmentation that the German theologian Paul Tillich used to describe the break-up of culture and society following the Second World War; rather, he used two striking metaphors, 'the shaking of the foundations' and 'existence on the boundaries'.[3] 'The shaking of the foundations' referred not only to the smoking ruins of – for example – the cities of Dresden and Hiroshima, which were the legacy of the Second World War, but to Tillich's conviction that the old expressions of the transcendence of God were useless, given the wholesale destruction he had witnessed, and the evils of the Holocaust which were only just beginning to be revealed in their full horror. He felt that the primitive and most essential foundations of our common life had been uprooted. So he evoked an experience of the presence of God as 'the Beyond in our midst', and as 'what concerned us ultimately'.[4] Furthermore, Tillich defined his own existence as being 'on the boundaries' – and it was not necessarily a creative position to hold! He was between old and new worlds, the old world of pre-World War Europe and the emerging new world in the United States; he was between the rational and the intuitive, between secular culture and religion – and Tillich is recognized as one of the first to blaze a trail for a creative interplay between the two and to follow the quest for the sacred in new cultural forms. He was – like his contemporary Dietrich Bonhoeffer – also on the boundaries between the established Church and the Confessing Church in Germany which had taken a stance against Nazism.[5] Even in our changed cultural situation this tension between establishment and radical prophetic Church is one which speaks to the position I opt for of *creative boundary living*. Yet again, the foundations of culture have been shaken as the century ends, the millennium looms and we try to make sense of a century which began – for Europe at least – with an assassination in Sarajevo, and is ending with a struggle to maintain a fragile peace in Bosnia. If, as the poet moaned, 'the centre does not hold',[6] the task is to discern what fragments can be gleaned to construct a new understanding of Church.

Fragmentation, then, is the principal metaphor I choose to describe the contemporary context,[7] a metaphor which operates on many levels. It appeals to the imagination, drawing together political and social developments, as well as the struggle to develop a spirituality which respects and integrates the human struggle for wholeness, amidst poverty and the pain of loss, amidst failure and anxiety for the future, even anxiety that there will be a future at all. *Fragmentation* as existential experience is firmly rooted in the Western spiritual tradition: it evokes the memory of Paul's struggles described in Romans 7:14–20 ('The evil that I would not, I do'), as well as the young Augustine's turmoil over his own sexuality. In the recurrent tensions between body and soul, in the desperation to flog the body into submission, the yearned-for wholeness has eluded the fragmented human personality. Even the more recent attempt of spirituality – feminist among others – to transcend the dreaded dualisms has resulted in us having no concept of soul, as Etty Hillesum remarked (in the quotation at the beginning of this section). To celebrate the body, unless grounded in a full-blown theology of spirit, is to lurch towards the danger of self-indulgent narcissism.

Lurching toward the millennium, *the foundations have again been shaken*. Fragmentation is experienced on a vast scale, as the political foundations of communism have been shaken in most of the East European countries.[8] Only the different versions of capitalism and the lure of the market economy are on offer to countries which have experienced a loss of vision and a collapsing into even greater spirals of debt, and moral turmoil. The boundaries where Tillich experienced tensions have acquired new – and sometimes sinister – meanings. The South/North divide has increased, and new groups of people have entered into positions of marginality, like people with AIDS, violated women forced from their homes, the gay communities and, on a global scale, refugees and asylum-seekers.

Fragmentation as a metaphor speaks to this political turmoil. It speaks to the desperate efforts of all those nations in Eastern Europe struggling for identity, visibility and for some solution to their desperate problems. In a recent dialogue, 'East meets West', a Czech woman theologian, Jana Opocenska, wrote to me: 'This civilization has reached its abyss in terms of extreme evil.'[9] Fragmentation speaks also to a situation where many people feel alienated from the democratic systems in which they participate: a growing sense of the erosion of democracy fosters this widespread alienation. 'It matters not which political party is in power' is a view frequently expressed. Encountering a homeless young person in the Underground station or on one of the bridges in our cities is to touch the meeting-point of many fragmentations – family, relationships, communities, the ghettoization of our cities, the social services, and the lack of compassion of the many passers-by, myself included. The only uniting factor in the situation is a shared helplessness – and accountability.

Fragmentation as a metaphor speaks also *philosophically* to a culture where we try to discover whether we are pre-modern, modern or post-modern – or indeed beyond postmodernism![10] The fragmentation of the great universalist constructions of Western European thought into smaller narratives with conflicting truth-claims highlights the question of the very possibility of truth and integrity where the spectre of relativism haunts. Where fragmentation reigns, the embodiment of mutuality, dialogue and understanding across the gulfs is increasingly problematic. In the women's movement the attempt to act in solidarity is frequently threatened by the splintering into groups identified by race, culture, sexual preference or religion. A reluctance to make the links between all these struggles for justice and to build an effective solidarity which respects identity and difference is an increasing problem and one which needs urgent addressing.

Just as fragmentation is experienced on many levels, there are many levels at which the situation is being addressed. The Christian Values in Europe Colloquium in Canterbury 1993 presented conflicting views as to what was the role of Christianity in confronting secularism, injustice and the vacuum in moral values.[11] Cardinal Daneels (Belgium) saw the response in terms of a unified ecumenical evangelism to turn Europe once more to Christ. The Anglican Archbishop of York, John Habgood, placed hope in Europe's traditions of commitment to human rights, revisiting the debate between Edward Burke and Tom Paine, and calling for a 'Christian realism' to be brought to the whole discussion and an avoidance of moral imperialism.[12] But both the former Irish Prime Minister Garret Fitzgerald and Professor James Mackey (Edinburgh University) challenged whether European Christianity had the necessary moral resources. As the latter remarked: 'Seen through the eyes of the post-colonized, Christian moral values may well seem less Christian, and perhaps less moral, than they seem through the eyes of post-imperial and less critical Europeans.'[13]

Despite the doubt thrown on the question as to whether European heritage – with its legacy of colonialism and religious and moral imperialism – could contribute anything to a culture of fragmentation, Garret Fitzgerald offered seeds of hope in suggesting that there were five revolutionary movements, four which are European in origin, which – it is my hope – could offer a way out of fragmentation and form a context for building a new theology of Church. He stressed the emergence in the Council of Europe of a concept of personal human rights which transcends the sovereignty of states; secondly, the emergence through the European Community of a profound rejection of war as an instrument of policy; thirdly, the abandonment by Europe of colonialism and the acceptance of the principle that the rich should *aid* the poor rather than *exploit* them; fourthly, the growth of ecological consciousness has created a new moral imperative and, fifthly, feminism has challenged the patriarchal norms on which our European civilization – with its Indo-European origins – is constructed.[14] Even if it is far from clear that war as an instrument has been abandoned, particularly helpful in both of these contributions was the calling into question of what we mean by 'European'. Increasingly Europe is defined in terms of a few dominant middle-European countries, excluding Eastern Europe and the poorer countries on the fringes.

So, to set against the seeds of hope which these five revolutionary movements offer, on a closer look at the roots of European culture it is a saddening experience to reflect that violence, and violence against women, is built into Europe's very origins. From its Greek roots was inherited Europe's very name, derived from an ancient Greek goddess Europa, the legendary daughter of the Phoenician king Agenor. She was raped by the father of the Greek gods, Zeus, who came to her in the form of a bull and carried her off to the island of Crete, where she bore him three sons. Thus did Europe acquire a name. The explanation of the four seasons in Greek myth is based on the rape of the goddess Persephone, daughter of the earth mother goddess, Demeter, by the god of the underworld, Pluto. The seasons of spring and summer are explained as the earth's rejoicing over the re-uniting of mother and daughter. And finally, the earliest example of connection between violence against women and war in Europe's history is offered by the Trojan War (c. 1200 BCE), which was ostensibly fought over the snatching of the beautiful Helen.[15] Economic violence against women is enshrined in stories and myths like those of Cinderella (the brothers Grimm), Gretchen (Goethe's *Faust*), the 'Little Match Girl' (Hans Andersen) and the 'poor women of the roads' of Celtic legend.

More directly linked to the present situation – and the backcloth to many of the discussions on 'the New Europe' – has been the espousing of the Christian myth as Europe's story, enshrined in the political, social and religious structure of Christendom.[16] The disastrous consequences for Jewish and Muslim communities of the dominant myth of 'Europe is the faith and the faith is Europe' (Hilaire Belloc) are at last beginning to act as a catalyst for a new conviction of the need for conversion and the urgency for ecumenical groups to be open to interfaith dialogue and action. Thus the dominant Christian myth has masked the cultural violence done to other faiths, in the name of Christian truth. Islam is still scapegoated as 'other' than what is authentically European. Dominant European Christianity – as the colonized Irish experience shows – has been and still is capable of suppressing the diversity of cultural groups. The Church's failure to play an effective role in the struggle for peace and reconciliation in Bosnia and in Northern Ireland is to some extent behind its present crisis of authority. Failure to take account of the violence built into Europe's structures has effectively blocked a way forward.

Hence the importance of the category of prophetic marginality as lighting a lamp out of the impasse. It has been highlighted by the Irish President Mary Robinson in her inaugural speech at Dublin Castle, in 1990, where she evoked the symbol of the fifth province of Ireland. Everyone knew it did not actually exist, but she evoked it in the sense of an empty space, a space for being open to the other in a posture of reconciliation: 'If I am a symbol of anything I would like to be a symbol of this reconciling and healing Fifth Province.'[17]

Why should it be Ireland leading Europe's way? In his book *Memory and Redemption*, Terence McCaughey showed one reason. Perhaps in the face of the level of suffering of Third World countries, from a small European country, with a history of being colonized and oppressed, comes a prophetic message which challenges the dominant European story. As he wrote:

Instead of meekly following the lead of the rather confused imperial powers as they seek a new post-imperial role in their policies towards e.g. South Africa . . . Ireland should without question be on the side of the exploited and be responding unilaterally as best as we can to the agonised calls they are sending out to us.[18]

This strengthens the hope expressed that the stance of prophetic marginality is what will move the Church forward. In a very different context it has been expressed by the theologians of El Salvador. All peoples marginalized through gender, race, class, physical or mental disability or sexual preference, from whatever society or country, have been called by the liberation theologian Jon Sobrino 'the crucified peoples'. Yet, in a recent lecture, his colleague from the University of Central America, the Jesuit Rodolfo Cardenal, showed how out of this fragmentation and brokenness springs a mighty hope for a renewal of culture.[19] The 'crucified peoples', he said, are the suffering servants of Yahweh: yet from them comes a powerful light which illuminates the shadow of our world.[20] Although they testify to the sin of the world, 'they offer the possibility of conversion as no other reality can offer it. The crucified people offer values that are not found anywhere else.'[21] The values which have such humanizing potential are '*community instead of individualism, service instead of egoism, simplicity instead of opulence, creativity instead of cultural mimicry, openness to transcendence instead of positivism and crass pragmatism*' (my italics). The crucified peoples embody a life of grace – a precious gift in a self-confessed atheistic culture – by showing that love and forgiveness are realities in a world that is structurally egoistic. But, it will be objected, this is language from Central America, not a recipe for a culture where 'I consume, therefore I am' increasingly defines identity, a culture where shopping and rushing for lottery tickets are the most popular hobbies.

Gathering the fragments: recovering psyche/soul

My suggestion is that in this fragmentation of culture, the task of *gathering the fragments* begins with listening to the excluded voices of those whom Cardenal calls 'the crucified peoples'. Only by listening to what we have excluded from the dominant myth of culture do we begin to create a language for the soul. For, as Etty Hillesum well knew, there is no collective language for the soul with which to challenge the prevailing value system. This is not only because of secularism, but because our understanding of *psyche/soul*[22] has shrunk to an over-individualized plane.

A theology of Church rests on the fact that Christian community exists for the care of souls, *cura animarum*, for the formation of caring and compassionate communities. Hence the task of soul-making, on personal, communal and socio-political levels, must be at the heart of becoming Church. From psychology has come the challenge – soul has shrunk to an individualistic irrelevance in the West. From that great giant of spirituality, Teilhard de Chardin, comes the reminder that:

> God wants only souls. To give those words their true value, we must not forget that the human soul, however independently created our philosophy represents it as being, is inseparable, in its birth and in its growth, from the universe into which it is born. In each soul, God loves and partly saves the whole world which that soul sums up in an incommunicable and particular way. But this summing-up, this welding, are not given to us ready-made and complete with the first awakening of consciousness. *It is we who, through our own activity, must industriously assemble the widely scattered elements . . .*
>
> Thus every man [sic!] . . . makes his own soul throughout all his earthly days; and at the same time he collaborates in another work, in another opus, which infinitely transcends, while at the same time it narrowly determines, the perspectives of his individual achievement: the completing of the world.[23] [My italics]

Gathering the widely scattered elements, making the connections as the work of soul-making, is exactly what I mean by *gathering the fragments* as the work of becoming Church in creating compassionate communities. But it is a work connecting the dimensions of interiority and the exterior work of justice-making. Women, confused and distressed by the order to 'lose their lives in order to find them', seen as the deepest value of the Gospel, have discovered the intimate connection between discovering a renewed sense of self (= soul), the search for just working conditions and the social revaluing of female sexuality. From the life of Etty Hillesum comes a blazing inspiration for what I call the task of creating 'landscapes for the soul'. Her story is told against the background of the gradual escalation of punitive measures of the SS against the Jews in Amsterdam, and the realization that total extermination was what lay in store for her, her family and those she loved. Her diaries record her transformation from being a pleasure-loving, mildly selfish and materialistic young woman into a profoundly spiritual person of great depth of love, joy and forgiveness:

> And here I have hit upon something essential: whenever I saw a beautiful flower, what I longed to do was to press it to my heart, or eat it all up. It was more difficult with a piece of beautiful scenery but the feeling was the same . . . I yearned physically for all I thought was beautiful, wanted to own it. Hence that

painful longing that could never be satisfied ... It all suddenly changed, God alone knows by what inner process, but it is different now.[24]

On the night when everything changed:

> I felt that God's world was beautiful despite everything, but its beauty now filled me with joy ... I went home invigorated and went back to work, and the scenery stayed with me in the background, as a cloak about my soul, to put it poetically, for once, but it no longer held me back.[25]

The transformation which she experienced was partly due to the powerful relationship with the psychotherapist Julius Spier, whom she loved passionately, but from whom she learnt to love deeply, without possessing. But this release into a power for loving and appreciation of the small details of living was achieved by connecting – the outer landscape with the inner. More explicitly, Etty Hillesum discovered a landscape for the soul:

> The train to Deventer. The open skies, peaceful and a little sad. I look out of the window and it is as if I were riding through the landscape of my own soul. Soul landscape. I feel like that often: that the outer landscape is a reflection of the inner ...[26]

Discovering a landscape for the soul did not mean that she became other-worldly, or developed a privatistic piety. But she laughingly described her own transformation from the girl who 'couldn't kneel', couldn't pray, wanted the love of Spier to herself, into a person who wanted to become prayer, who had developed contemplation into a way of being. Greater awareness brought access to her inner resources. The ability to connect inner with outer drove her to wrestle with the terrible evils which were the context for her personal struggle:

> Something has crystallised. I have looked at our destruction, our miserable end which has already begun in so many small ways in our daily life straight in the eye, and accepted it into my life, and my love of life has not been diminished ... I continue to grow from day to day, even with the likelihood of destruction staring me in the face.[27]

The prophetic element of speaking as one of the 'crucified people' for Etty Hillesum meant that she let death into her life and was enriched by it. It goes without saying that she condemned the transportations, worsening humiliations, the physical and mental cruelties: but the ability to create a landscape for the soul, connecting the political conditions with inner growth, was a special gift:

The jasmine outside my house has been completely ruined by the rains and storms of the last few days, its white blossoms are floating about on muddy black pools on the low garage roof. But somewhere inside me the jasmine continues to blossom undisturbed, just as profusely and delicately as it ever did. And it spreads its scent around the house in which you dwell, O God.[28]

Her second inspiration was her refusal to hate the Nazis. Rather, she wanted to be the 'thinking heart of the concentration camp', to anticipate some of the great suffering in store, to suffer for the vulnerable, and to act as balm for all hatred. This is exactly what Rodolfo Cardenal meant by embodying grace and forgiveness. Rich interior landscapes are given external meaning in the redemptive healing of the social situation.

This inspiring story of 'soul-making', I believe, can call feminist and other liberation spiritualities of the North and West to a neglected dimension, yet a dimension often vibrant in the spirituality of women of colour, as the other quotation at the beginning of this chapter, from *A Troubling in My Soul*, indicates. In many of these communities, despite the oppressions of slavery and colonialism, psyche/soul/spirit has not been eclipsed. But before exploring this dimension of soul-making as an ecclesial task, I want to open up the traditional ways of thinking about Church, to discover why they so provide such little inspiration for this culture of fragmentation.

Notes

1 Gerard Manley Hopkins, 'Justus quidem tu es, Domine' in *Gerard Manley Hopkins, Poems and Prose* (Harmondsworth: Penguin Classics, 1953), p. 67.

2 Hannah Ward and Jennifer Wild, *Guard the Chaos* (London: Darton, Longman and Todd, 1995).

3 Paul Tillich, *The Shaking of the Foundations* (1959; London: Pelican, 1962).

4 Tillich, ibid.

5 It is impossible to ignore the fact that Tillich is an ambiguous figure for feminists, as Hannah Tillich has pointed out in her biography, *From Time to Time* (New York: Stein and Day, 1973). Yet the usefulness of a concept like 'existence on the boundaries' to feminist theology is clear from Mary Daly's analysis in *Beyond God the Father* (Boston: Beacon, 1973). Daly makes quite clear what are its limitations.

6 William Butler Yeats, 'The Second Coming' in *Collected Poems* (London: Macmillan, 1965), pp. 210–11.

7 In *The Wisdom of Fools?* (London: SPCK, 1993) I described this as a *culture of separation*. But since then the process of separating has taken several steps further so that splitting, fragmenting are now more accurate descriptions. I have worked on these ideas in 'A vanished integrity? Epiphanies of grace in a fragmented world' (The Anne Spencer Memorial Lecture, Bristol, 1994); 'The shaking of the foundations – again!' (The Von Hügel Lecture, Cambridge, 1994).

8 I am aware that this is a generalization, that communism seems to be regaining some lost ground in Russia and that ex-communists won the recent elections in Poland.

9 Mary Grey and Jana Opocenska, *Yearbook of the European Society of Women in Theological Research* 1 (August 1993), pp. 68–83.

10 See John Millbank, 'Problematising the secular: the post, postmodern agenda' in *Shadows of Spirit: Postmodernism and Religion*, ed. Philippa Berry and Andrew Wernick (London and New York: Routledge, 1992), pp. 30–44.

11 See Grace Davie, Robin Gill and Stephen Platten (eds), *Christian Values in Europe* (Cambridge: Christianity and the Future of Europe, 1993).

12 Ibid., pp. 20–33.

13 Ibid., p. 69.

14 Garret Fitzgerald, ibid., p. 58.

15 I have developed this in ' "Weep not for me but for yourselves and for your children": The search for integrity in a culture of violence' (William Hudson Memorial Lecture, Cardiff, May 1995).

16 See M. Grey, 'Insiders and outsiders: women and Europe' in *Insiders and Outsiders: On the Making of Europe*, ed. Jürgen Wiersma (Kampen: Kok Pharos, 1995), pp. 24–38.

17 See Fergus Finlay, *Mary Robinson: A President with a Purpose* (Dublin: The O'Brien Press, 1990), p. 156.

18 Terence McCaughey, *Memory and Redemption: Church Politics and Prophetic Theology in Ireland* (Dublin: Gill & Macmillan, 1993), pp. 118–19.

19 Rodolfo Cardenal SJ, 'The crucified peoples' in *Reclaiming Vision: Education, Liberation and Justice*, Papers of the Inaugural Summer School (Centre for Contemporary Theology, LSU College, Southampton, July 1994), pp. 12–18.

20 Ibid., p. 17.

21 Ibid.

22 This will be explained in a mythic way in Chapter 3.

23 Pierre Teilhard de Chardin, *Le Milieu Divin* (London: William Collins Sons and New York: Harper and Brothers, 1960), pp. 31–2.

24 Etty Hillesum, *An Interrupted Life: The Diaries of Etty Hillesum 1941–3* (New York: Washington Square Press, 1981), p. 13.

25 Ibid.

26 Ibid., p. 8.

27 Ibid., p. 12.

28 Ibid., p. 188.

2

THE DREAM OF A COMMON LANGUAGE

There we were – conservative evangelicals and honest agnostics and liberal Methodists and fun-loving feminists and socially-engaged Buddhists – dancing to Jewish folk-songs, . . . imaginatively returning divine sparks to heaven with flicks of our fingers . . . As we were dancing . . . on that hot summer's day, I had the feeling that I was experiencing what Christians call church, Buddhists call *sangha*, and what fun-loving feminists call community. I had the feeling I was participating in the divine communion, in God. Regardless of personal philosophy or life orientation, every dancer had a place. Even the birds joined in; even the grass . . .

(Jay McDaniel[1])

This is an intuition which many of us can share. Even if I want to push to one side the stereotype about 'fun-loving feminists', I too have had glimpses of such a rich experience of Christian community in vastly different settings – on a mountainside, at Taizé, in Christian feminist liturgies, ecumenical house-groups, family house-masses celebrated by my brother (a Catholic priest), the funerals of my mother and father, the ordination of the women priests at Lichfield Cathedral – so that I cannot just abandon hope in this, the Dark Night of the Church. Even if the accusation that the Church is acting as 'guardian of the silenced' rings true, against that has to be set the lived reality of thousands of ordinary people who receive nurture and inspiration from the celebration of the liturgical seasons, from active Christian discipleship, from the 'divine communion' to which Jay McDaniel alluded, and from the actual experience of the Spirit gracing their lives in Christian community – people who know ourselves called to be the 'Community of the Beloved', the Beloved Community. It is the argument of this chapter that the categories in which the meaning of Church is discussed are deadlocked. It is simply not helpful to revisit those well-rehearsed battlegrounds of 'charism or institution?', of categories of membership ('Who is in or who is out?'), 'Outside the Church there is no salvation' (*extra ecclesiam nulla salus*), the seeming tyranny of magisterial authority, the tensions around the celibacy of the clergy – at this stage, at least. There is a deeper level at which the question should be addressed.

For, if the intuitions of the last chapter are correct, that what people cry out for in a culture of fragmentation is the *gathering of the fragments* in the activity of soul-making as a personal and communal task for society, then the question becomes, is the Church equal to this task? Has is not come adrift on the quicksands of legalism and hierarchical management? And more fundamentally still, does a common language exist for what we actually mean by Church? Is there even the 'dream of a common language'?[2] If we were to share perceptions and images of Church, we would discover not a common language, but an enormous spectrum of interpretations of Church.[3]

Is there a common language of 'being Church'?

The first spectrum of interpretations would be between the two polarities: from discipleship seen in direct continuity with the ragged band of Jesus' original followers, and perhaps manifested in many basic communities of *campesinos* in the barrios of Latin and Central America, to membership of a highly organized institution, where liturgy and personal morality are strictly regulated. It would be easy and false to caricature this contrast as being that of the Church of the people and the Church of the clergy. Zeffirelli did exactly that, in his film *Brother Sun, Sister Moon*, where he pictured the clergy of Assisi at High Mass in the Duomo, with rich vestments and jewel-encrusted fingers – but in an empty Cathedral! And where were the people? Down in the valley with Francis and Clare, in a warm huddle around the altar with their goats, hens and sheep, as they celebrated an enthusiastic eucharist to the strains of twentieth-century guitars! Very much Sixties picaresque ... and authentic to a certain type of experience of Church. But the caricature lies in ignoring the complexity of the current scene, where it might well be the *parents* of the young people clustering around the popular style, while their offspring look either for the formal liturgies of high Catholicism, or the structured enthusiasm of evangelicalism. The caricature also does scant justice to the very real attempts by all the mainstream churches to achieve a balanced worship in terms of both traditional styles and contemporary relevance.

This leads precisely to the second spectrum, namely the range of positions from conservative evangelical, to liberal, to conservative, traditional or progressive versions of 'catholicism'. This is of course most evident in the Anglican Church, but has its parallels in Roman Catholicism. As the liberal position of the Sixties and Seventies seemed to gain ground, and universalism and ultimate claims seemed to be given up in favour of relativism and contextual versions of truth, so there has been a rush to the apparent securities of either conservative evangelicalism or 'high' catholicism. This search for certainty and security was also fuelled by a reaction to what has been seen as the 'threat of feminism' and 'New Age' – with an ignoring of the complexity and diversity of positions represented by these two movements. Many of these conservative positions represent a creeping fundamentalism, which has itself added fire to the backlash against feminism and 'New Age'. Thus it was possible to fuel the arguments against the ordination of women in the Church of England from both an evangelical and a catholic spectrum, making it easy to avoid facing the underlying misogyny of both wings.

A third spectrum of understandings of Church is the range represented by the house-church movements.[4] Although the largest – and ever-increasing – grouping of these might be loosely termed evangelical, there does not seem to be an easily-definable category within which all can be subsumed. Many represent a new flowering of what their members imagine the original New Testament household churches to have been. This can result in a defensive attitude to 'the world' and a self-definition over against it. Many of these groups would regard themselves as charismatic, although one could also point to charismatic wings within many of the mainstream churches. But another group of 'house-churches' is more easily described as house-groups or cells within larger churches; these frequently represent Christians seeking a more intimate manner of fellowship through prayer, shared worship and meals, but they also cover a range of groups who might come under my definition of 'prophetic-marginal', since they include numerous Justice and Peace groups (mentioned in the Introduction) who consider themselves very much the progressive – critical, questioning yet loyal – wing of the contemporary churches. Jim Wallis's Sojourners Community in Washington, DC fits easily into the category of prophetic-marginal, yet it is an evangelical community thoroughly inclusive of all movements for justice. In fact Sojourners gives the first clue to what might be the common factor of prophetic Church – that it bursts the wineskins, demanding new categories or *no restrictive categories* for the demands of proclaiming the Gospel.[5]

The fourth spectrum is the focus of this book. It is the exploration of the Christian community as *prophetically marginal, as the place for creative boundary-living*: it is witnessed to by glimpses from many of the groups mentioned above. It is also represented by the Women-Church movement.[6] This is prophetic in its assertion that the Church as 'discipleship of equals' is faithful to the original inspiration of the Jesus movement, a position outlined already in 1980 by

Elisabeth Schüssler Fiorenza.[7] This working definition has itself now developed to include a spectrum of meanings, from exodus from institutional Church (Mary Daly), exodus specifically from alienating forms of Church (Rosemary Ruether), to base-communities of justice-seeking friends (Mary Hunt), and to the idea of a space, open yet bounded, where diverse communities of women and justice-seeking men are in dialogue with each other and with other faith communities (Schüssler Fiorenza and others).

The question then arises: what is the uniting factor which makes the word 'church' appropriate and justifiable?[8] For *prophetic marginality* cannot by self-definition alone win the day. It is essential that Christian community springs from faith in Jesus Christ and historical continuity with that faith – in a range of positions, from seeing Jesus as distant charismatic, prophetic healer, to cosmic Lord of history, eucharistically and sacramentally present, with many distinctions in between. 'Where there is following of Christ, there is Church' – and not the other way around, necessarily – was the way I was taught ecclesiology.[9] But the corollary of this is never faced, namely, that where there is institutional Church, there is not necessarily authentic discipleship of Christ. This challenge was depicted dramatically by Nikos Kazantzakis, in his novel *Christ Recrucified*.[10] When a small village in Greece casts the parts for its Passion play, the part of Christ falls to young Manolios, a shepherd boy. As all the characters, amazingly, grow into the parts for which they were cast, a ragged band of refugees arrives in their village, begging for food and shelter. This is denied them – and the refusal springs from the village leaders and all the official dignitaries of the church. Only Manolios and a small band of friends go into the mountains with the refugees and struggle with them to ward off starvation. It is a struggle which ends with the murder of Manolios – yes, at the foot of the cross in the village church. Here, Kazantzakis is saying, *there was Church, but no true following of Christ*.

'Following Christ – but which Christ are we following?' is therefore a crucial question. And traditional theologies of Church have all tried to answer this in various ways. The Church as the Body of Christ, the Sacrament of Christ, is a frequent base for ecclesiology.[11] For twenty years, the approach of Avery Dulles towards understanding Church has been popular. Utilizing the current popularity of models as a heuristic device in science, Dulles proposed, as models for the Church, institution, community, sacrament, servant and herald. These were to a large extent mirrors of the theology of the Second Vatican Council, where the Church as the pilgrim people of God came to be seen as the most popular image. His book was widely adopted – even outside Roman Catholic circles – and even though he himself is critical of some of its stresses, it remains influential.

There is no doubt that there is still much mileage to be gained from most of these suggestions. Of course the Church needs government, is struggling to be authentic community, to mediate Christ's presence, to be servant of the poor and oppressed and to proclaim the Gospel. As the Church of sinners it will never fully embody its ideals in this world. So why is there such widespread alienation? It cannot be the models themselves, but the lack of fit between them – or similar ones – and the lived experience of people. The Church as institution appears more often to silence the individual and to exclude the experience of the very people who should have privileged place in the Kingdom of God. The Church as Sacrament makes insufficient links with movements for justice, and fails to earth itself in ecological realities. Sacraments can also be effective in building up formal institutional elements of Church; yet in doing so may give the impression that the Church possesses the dispensing of the Holy Spirit, controls the mystery of the Spirit and is several degrees removed from the lived practice of enspirited faith.[12] The Church as herald, charged with the mission of the proclamation of the Gospel, has entangled this mission in its own power structures. All too often proclamation, instead of being seen as the baptismal commitment of every individual, is understood as flowing from inflexible decrees of the magisterium (in the Roman Catholic Church at least), from which there can be no dissent. The idea that Europe must re-group around the old idea of Christendom – which has emerged from the agenda of the Decade of Evangelization – is one example of this. It seems that no links have been made between the privileged position of Christianity in Europe and the silence over the murder of the Jews during the Holocaust. It is my hope that, as we approach the millennium, the theme of reconciliation proclaimed by John Paul II in his Apostolic Letter *Tertio Millennio Adveniente* will include humility and the Church's repenting of decisions responsible for many of the tragedies of history.

Four dimensions of Church revisited

Would it be a more helpful starting-point to take the four dimensions, *diakonia* (service), *leitourgia* (worship), *koinonia* (community) and, again, *proclamation* of the Word, as constitutive of being Church?[13] As with the models which Dulles offered, there is absolutely nothing wrong with these dimensions of Church – in fact they are crucial. But in many instances the way they are understood fails to make an impact on the structures of society in which they are lived. To proclaim *diakonia* as the essence of Church, and to take scant notice of the position of women as servants, even slaves, paid atrociously, forced into sexual slavery in many parts of the world, is to make *diakonia* an ideology which is simply out of touch. To make this worse, the spirituality of following Christ the poor man, *servus servorum*, servant of the very poorest, locks women (and poor men) in many parts of the world into acceptance of oppressive situations, where service is not caring and compassion, but enforced humiliation in order to survive. To take the example of the Korean and other 'comfort women' is perhaps an extreme instance of this,[14] but in this contemporary entrepreneurial society caring professions are in general rated very low on the ladder and it is women who bear the brunt of the injustice. 'Service' carries a range of meanings, from sex tourism to cleaning office blocks late at night; or it has been caught up into the 'customer service' jargon, where the world is divided into paying customers and entrepreneurial businesses offering their 'services' – at a competitive price. It simply adds to the suffering, injustice and sense of being trapped, when Church documents proclaim that women are by nature more 'caring', docile, and all those qualities subsumed under the word 'feminine'.[15] What is to me tragic, is that the ministry of deacon – ministry of service *par excellence* – could in fact be of profound significance as a response to these tragic circumstances, *were service to be understood as including a dimension of mutuality and reciprocity, where carers, too, are worthy of dignity and acknowledged to have needs.*

In a society where we are frequently treated to gloom-and-doom statistics about falling numbers and empty churches, it is cold comfort to be told that the essence of Church is *leitourgia*, worship. And yet I want to cling to the dimension of *worship* as something infinitely precious. There is already something counter-cultural about using words like *adoration* and *worship*. But if we were honest about our society, it is the false gods of wealth and the life which money buys that are worshipped and adored. As a nation Britain is enthusiastic about TV programmes such as *Songs of Praise*. Yet a recent study of the hymns sung on this programme reveals that the images of God most popularly presented reinforce the traditional, patriarchal concepts summarized by Brian Wren as KINGAFAP, in other words, God imaged as King-God-Almighty-Father-Protector.[16] In other words, the kind of worship which attracts even those who would never set foot in a church will reinforce traditionally held beliefs, will comfort and not disturb the *status quo*. Moreover, in a sinister way, unobserved by most people, the monuments of the consumerist society – the grand hypermarkets and shopping malls springing up everywhere in Europe and North America – are mimicking the architecture of the emptying cathedrals in a kind of demonic parody. Why do we not notice that many supermarkets are even being built in the shape of cathedrals, with domes or spires? And that on entering these palaces, one is greeted with music, art, green foliage (artificial)? There is entertainment, liturgies of the word (advertisement) and plenty of tasting of free samples. Desires are kindled and senses awakened. The *eros* of accumulation of loaded trollies increases, until the climax of the encounter at the cash till is reached. Ian Linden, General Secretary of CIIR, once called this 'the great sacramental act' of today. These are the lived realities around the empty churches. This is the world where instead of the Sunday church liturgy, many people have filled their lives with the liturgies of the Sunday shopping, the rituals of car-washing and buying the Sunday newspaper, as well as endless TV.

And what of *koinonia*, community? In a world where it is possible to find *virtual* community on the Internet?[17] In a society where self-interested individualism reigns? It is precisely the deeply held conviction that *community* is vital to being human that prevents many people from abandoning the Church, and is the reason why this book is written. The very superficiality and shallowness of so many forms of association keeps sparking the search for genuine community which will nurture soul-making. The activity of *gathering the fragments* reveals that where people find the kind of community which addresses their needs, they will accept discipline and live out a fidelity to the group which is giving them new hope. For example, the twelve-step programme of Alcoholics Anonymous, and the family of such groups which respond to different sorts of addiction, provide the structured support which the Church once gave, and are based on a real faith in divine power.[18] In a similar way, parents of a handicapped child, sufferers from a rare disease, people caring for the terminally ill, find strength and community in forming support groups which lead them deeper into a spiritual exploration. For there is no lack of new forms of associations and clubs: it would seem that nothing will crush the human need to find satisfying forms of relating.

It is the focus of all of these which needs attention. Do people come together in this consumer society more to find the answer to an immediate need than inspired by a common ideal? Years of struggling to find support for Third World action groups have shown me that this is frequently the case. It was noticeable that when a counselling group sprang up in the area which I lived, 300 people immediately turned up to join what was on offer. Counselling meets the immediate emotional needs in the way that working to eradicate someone else's poverty does not. It is certainly obvious that what people want is a form of community where they experience meaningful participation. It is questionable whether the large parish grouping, for which the formal Sunday liturgy is the chief expression, can ever satisfy this need; nor can it nurture idealism.

Many people who responded to the opportunities of the times by becoming educated in theology, by actively pursuing a life of faith through membership of different groups, unless they are extraordinarily lucky, will find the Sunday service an exercise in monumental boredom, perpetuating a theology of Church which they have long left behind. Yet in the Roman Catholic Church, the priest can be seen as much a victim of the situation as laypeople themselves. He may not be a good preacher, yet he must preach. He may not be much of a theologian, yet he must theologize. He is, by definition at least, celibate – yet must tell married people how to lead their sexual lives. This is the situation from which many young people have chosen to walk out.

For all this, the search for true *koinonia* is not yet quenched. *Where there is following of Christ, there is Church* – as I said earlier – and one of the amazing features of the Christ event is that it casts its spell anew across the centuries. No one could have predicted, for example, that Mahatma Gandhi, with a Hindu background (although influenced by Jainism and Buddhism), would have found his own inspiration for non-violence from Jesus' preaching of the Kingdom. And yet he came to the Sermon on the Mount indirectly, through the influence of Tolstoy.[19] There is a clue here as to what could be the true meaning of *the proclamation of the Word*, which was the fourth dimension of Church. There is no need to be bogged down by what appears often to be official teaching from which there can be no deviation: it is the way in which the Gospel inspiration is communicated and lived in the lives of people of faith – all faiths – which is crucial. *Less of the image of the trumpet from the ramparts is needed, and more of the image of the yeast which leavens the bread, and the mustard seed which grows from small beginnings.*

But surely, it will be objected, we have a reliable identification for the true Church? Is she not one, holy, catholic and apostolic? The last section of this chapter explores whether, after all, this – the place of the four traditional marks of the Church – is the place to start.

How shall we know Christ's Church?

The challenge of unity for the Christian Church today is not to bewail the flagging energies of the ecumenical movement, which is where people point when asked why the Church is not united. Through the Churches Together movement there is enormous goodwill and energy at a local level, even if this has not been matched by doctrinal agreement about eucharist and ordination. The challenge is rather that the churches focus energies on a common witness against injustice and unite in struggling to find solutions in the tragic conflict areas of the world. To that end it is heartening that the Conference of European Churches (CEC) and the Council of European Bishops' Conferences (CCEE) have adopted the theme of 'Reconciliation: Gift of God and Source of New Life' for their next Assembly in 1997.[20] People are no longer impressed if groups of Christians can come together at certain times of the year, sing hymns and make civil noises to each other, if in many parts of the world Christians are at each other's throats. The Secretary General of the World Council of Churches, the Revd Conrad Raiser, has himself hinted that the old paradigm for ecumenism has had its day: simply to believe that by endless talking break-through on doctrinal issues will be achieved no longer holds water.[21] In a manner reminiscent of the five revolutions mentioned by Garret Fitzgerald (see Chapter 1), Conrad Raiser hinted that a new paradigm would have to take into account justice both for women and for the earth. But the second factor calling for new considerations on Christian unity is the question of the dominant role which the Christian story has played in colonial history and how this is to be addressed when working for just international relations. This strikes at the heart of what we mean by Christian truth and is the major stumbling block in making peace with the great world religions.

For example, Stanley Hauerwas, in full recognition of this difficulty, quotes Lesslie Newbigin as saying:

> Christians can never seek refuge in a ghetto where their faith is not proclaimed as public truth for all. They can never agree that there is one law for themselves and another for the world. They can never admit that there are orders of creation or powers or dominions that exist otherwise than to serve Christ.[22]

Hauerwas' answer to this, the difficulty of proclaiming the story as the truth, without underwriting patterns of domination, is to advocate the telling of the story, in the hope that in its embodiment will be the salvation which comes from God. It is to his credit that he publishes (as an appendix) a challenge to his position by a graduate student who cites the position of a friend who pleads the cause of the Sioux Indians, their values, their truth. The friend challenges: 'Is there not a violence already implicit in the conviction that one possesses the truth?' and asks how a Sioux Indian would react to Newbigin's view. Hauerwas does not answer the challenge – but Christianity must, if the 'unity' which Christ longed for is to be a healing force in the world.

It is with the question 'how is the Church holy?' that the greatest stumbling blocks are encountered. Rather than list a catalogue of accusations of scandalous abuse of power and trust and refusal to listen to any voice of dissent, I pose the challenge: *What do people of faith understand by holiness today, and how would they imagine that embodied in an institution?* I sense a global groundswell of longing from people of goodwill that an institution which in name stands for truth and justice should be acknowledged as a beacon of hope in a culture given up to greed and violence. The conviction is still strong that the discipleship marked by the Resurrection story of Jesus is a valid and enriching way to live and is a life-enhancing path to God. But even if there are many faces of the Church which seem to be a counter-symbol to this, the belief that the Church is holy is the very reason why so many Christians take a stance of loyal dissent and criticism. 'They will not hijack my Church', as Rosemary Radford Ruether — and others — have cried! She even alludes to the possibility that, when the face of holiness has been obscured, the faithful remnant must embark on an exodus journey, but not alone, for God will be our companion: 'We are not in exile, but the Church is in exodus with us. God's Shekinah, Holy Wisdom, the Mother-face of God has fled from the high thrones of patriarchy and has gone into exodus with us.'[23]

It is not difficult to point to *personal* icons of holiness today and it is not my purpose to do so. It is not in doubt here that there are wonderful examples of this. The challenge is rather that there should be a clear *institutional witness of holiness* as a challenge to individualistic materialism. As I write, it is the week of the funeral of Archbishop Derek Worlock of Liverpool. It is undeniable that in his work of confronting poverty and racism in the inner city, together with the Anglican Bishop, David Sheppard, there was a startling witness to holiness presented by the public face of the Church. (Although, inevitably, some have tried to deny this.) It is also true that the concerted action of the churches to oppose the government's Asylum Bill and, a few years earlier, the united action against homelessness are also public witnesses to the fact that 'the Church is holy'. When people of many faiths walk the streets together in a pilgrimage searching for peace, or pray for reconciliation in Northern Ireland, this is another sign of hope. That Church-funded agencies — like CAFOD and Christian Aid — are tackling the root causes of poverty in the Third World and at home is also a crucial part of this witness of holiness.

Holiness can never be a static notion but reflects the way the Spirit of God is at work in the age. One of the lessons which secularism teaches is that God is at work in myriad ways outside official Church structures. Icons of sacred living are found in surprising places, suggesting that the heart of being Church *meaningfully* is a shifting category, refusing to be bound by regulations. I note three aspects, briefly, as each will be developed later.

Creation spirituality in its variety of expressions invites the discovery of the sacred through celebrating the connections with the rhythms of the seasons, with nature in all her moods: even the harshness of winter's cold conceals hidden growth. There is a holiness in attending patiently to the revelation of each season in succession, the mystery of death and rebirth, an attitude of wonder and receptivity which was formerly associated with Christian liturgy. The holiness of time and space is very much part of this. Secondly, there is holiness, too, in fidelity to the stance of resistance to injustice from the margins: this demands the courage to be alone, to face criticism and humiliation by the very institution from which one hoped the face of the Crucified and Risen One would shine. It is a 'political' holiness. Thirdly, the recovery of the meaning of holiness as 'wholeness' has encouraged the development of an embodied spirituality, where the sacredness of relating to God and to each other in the goodness of bodily and sexual feeling is celebrated in an attempt to recover from the over-spiritualized approach of centuries. Karl Rahner wrote movingly of the spirituality needed for our times, in fact, the plurality of spiritualities necessary – which he thought was far away from an over-reliance on the cult of altar sacrifices. If a believer takes responsibility for 'his' own life, he said, then there is today a spirituality, a Christ.[24]

But the difficulty with institutional holiness may be that Christianity seeks a too sharply delineated view of purity and innocence. Grappling with the forces of evil within the structures forces us to leave the moral high ground of being 'untainted', the innocence of non-involvement. Is the price of struggling against institutional evil and structural sin a concept of holiness which is far removed from plaster-cast saints and established icons? Ambiguity, the calling into question of established norms, even those of respectability and order – could this be the path where holiness is not sought, but found? Perhaps, in this dark night, the only way it can be found?

How should the Church be 'catholic' today? One kind of answer is certainly being given through the number of Anglicans joining the Roman Catholic Church, although this trail is less than had been anticipated during the storm which followed the ordination of women in the Church of England; it has also been balanced by an exodus in the opposite direction. Catholicism is also understood as 'the catholic wing' of the Church of England, that dimension which considers itself most akin to the Church of Rome in liturgy, theology and general sympathies. It was this 'wing' which was most upset that the decision to ordain women had been made without the will of the Church as a whole being united behind it. But what is usually meant by 'catholic' is that the truth of the Catholic Church is universally applicable in all times and all places. It is this conviction which for centuries set missionaries on fire to win the world for Christ, and has continued to fuel prejudices against 'the heathen'.

This history has to be placed against the backcloth I sketched in Chapter 1, namely the climate of postmodernism and the 'shaking of the foundations' where the political hegemony which underpinned colonialism and the style of missionary activity which accompanied it have been challenged and in many places successfully overcome.[25] One only has to think about the immensely successful film *The Mission*, based on the historical mission of the Jesuits in Paraguay. The story hinged on two styles of resistance, armed and violent (represented by the radical priest, Rodrigo), and a non-violent resistance (led by Gabriel, also a Jesuit, holding the monstrance on high). That both styles end in tragic failure is not the point here: rather, both these Jesuits were totally committed to the people in their struggles to survive and to eke out a meagre living. It is echoed today in many parts of the world. For example, the Columban Missionary Congregation now publishes a well-loved newsletter, *Vocation for Justice*, where it is clear that if there is a universal truth it is the need for commitment to justice and hunger for justice in the particular poor country where one works, but *on the terms of the people there*, not in terms of thrusting a Eurocentric catholicism or protestantism on the local population.

Yet this cannot be the total answer to the meaning of catholicity: commitment to justice cannot renege on the conflicting claims of doctrinal truth. On the one hand there is today the increasing tendency – seen in the documentation from the magisterium, the encyclicals, the new Catechism and the manner in which these demand unflinching obedience from the faithful – to proclaim catholic truth with an unmistakable clarity; on the other hand, we encounter the problem alluded to by Stanley Hauerwas – see above – where the insistence on the eternal truth-claims of Christianity eliminated respect for truth in the lives of the Sioux Indians. The whole validity of the attempt to build bridges with other faiths hangs in the balance here. It is entirely understandable that people today find the endless relativism and shifting sands of postmodernism cold comfort and refuse to accept that 'the centre does not hold'. The insecurities of 'the shaking of the foundations' have always produced this reaction. The question is: does complete acceptance of truth, universally valid, dogmatically enshrined in one particular way, foreclose on a deeper spiritual quest, a profounder notion of catholicity?

Is this profounder notion what awaits us at the other end of the Dark Night? This book will attempt to plumb the depths of this darkness.

Does a deeper notion of what apostolicity also might mean also await us at the end of the Dark Night? The criterion of unbroken succession from Peter onwards continues to be one interpretation of this. But it also exists in conjunction with deeper – and not necessarily conflicting – notions. As Hans

Küng wrote nearly thirty years ago, and his words have an extraordinary freshness for today:

> Apostolicity ... must be continually achieved afresh, must be a recurring event in a living history which occurs between the Church and the apostles, between the Church's teaching and the apostles' witness, between the church's ministry and the apostles' commission. ... Apostolicity is not something that can be simply stated and proved in theory. The Church must share in this history in order to recognize and understand, to experience and discover what the apostolicity of the Church means. As an individual Christian, I must become a true successor of the apostles, I must hear their witness, believe their message, imitate their mission and ministry. I must be, and always become anew, a believing and living member of the apostolic community. Only then shall I understand what it means when I say and confess: *credo apostolicam ecclesiam*.[26]

To answer the question as to what could be the particular quality and criteria of apostolicity, seen as the charism and responsibility of the entire Christian Church which cannot be reduced to merely episcopal succession in time (while recognizing the bishops and Church leaders as key figures of responsibility in this), a whole new way of thinking about Church is needed. Only by facing honestly the degree of confusion and disillusion, loss of heart, and shame which so many ordinary people feel when scandal and corruption are discovered in the Church's midst, can we glimpse light in the Dark Night. What could be the building blocks to move us forward?

Notes

1 Jay McDaniel, *With Roots and Wings: Christianity in an Age of Ecology and Dialogue* (Maryknoll: Orbis, 1995), p. viii.

2 *The Dream of a Common Language* is the title of a collection of poems by Adrienne Rich (New York: W. & W. Norton, 1978).

3 The following categorization is meant to be impressionistic and is a heuristic tool – not a sociological survey – simply to enable us to get a handle on what exactly Church means for Christians today, and why it has such an alienation and embittering effect on so many people. I am aware, for example, that I have not discussed the movement from sect to church, as classically discussed by Troeltsch, partly because I see new configurations of this.

4 See Andrew Walker, *Restoring the Kingdom* (London: Hodder and Stoughton, 1987).

5 For a better idea of the commitments of Sojourners, to read the titles of the journal is itself educative. For a glimpse of its prophetic potential, see Jim Wallis, *The Soul of Politics: Beyond 'Religious Right' and 'Secular Left'* (San Diego and New York: Harcourt Brace and Co., 1994).

6 The literature on Women-Church is now vast. See Rosemary Radford Ruether, *Women-Church: Theology and Practice* (New York: Harper and Row, 1990); Elisabeth Schüssler

Fiorenza, *Discipleship of Equals: An Ecclesialogy of Liberation* (New York: Crossroads, 1993); M. Grey, *The Wisdom of Fools?* (London: SPCK, 1993), ch. 9; Letty Russell, *Church in the Round* (Louisville, KY: Westminster, John Knox, 1993).

7 Elisabeth Schüssler Fiorenza, *In Memory of Her* (London: SCM, 1980).

8 In Women-Church debates it is frequently objected that the very word 'church' is itself alienating.

9 By Professor T. J. Van Bavel, the Augustinian scholar, at the Faculty of Theology, Leuven, Belgium.

10 N. Kazantzakis, *Christ Recrucified*, tr. Jonathan Griffin (London: Faber and Faber, 1962).

11 See Avery Dulles, *Models of Church* (Dublin: Gill and Macmillan, 1976); *A Church to Believe in: Discipleship and the Dynamics of Freedom* (New York: Crossroads, 1983); Edward Schillebeeckx, *Christ, the Sacrament of the Encounter with God* (London: Sheed and Ward, 1963).

12 I do not for one moment want to decry the efforts to revive the catechumenate and to work for sacramental renewal. See M. Grey, A Heaton and D. Sullivan (eds), *The Candles Are Still Burning: New Directions in Sacrament and Spirituality* (London: Geoffrey Chapman, 1995). Nor do I underestimate the new enthusiasm for the Alpha programmes which are currently attracting many young people.

13 This is the approach taken, for example, by Cardinal Hume, in *Searching for God* (London: Hodder and Stoughton, 1977).

14 The keynote speech at the dialogue between women theologians from South and North, called together by the Ecumenical Association of Third World Theologians (EATWOT), was given by Chung Hyun Kyung, 'Your comfort versus my death', and focused on the plight of the 'comfort women' of Korea and the struggle for survival of one, Soo Bock. See MaryJohn Mananzan, Mercy Oduyoye, Elsa Tamez, Shannon Clarkson, Mary Grey and Letty Russell (eds), *Women Resisting Violence: A Spirituality for Life* (Maryknoll: Orbis, 1996), pp. 129–40.

15 See *The Tablet* correspondence (10 and 17 February, 1996) for examples of this essentialist language. Fr Peter Milward SJ declared his opinion that women were too good to be priests: whereupon, in her reply the following week, Monica Furlong said that, at the end of the nineteenth century, when women were trying to set up a house of learning at Oxford, the Anglican Bishop Wordsworth told them to stop it because they were *too good for education!*

16 See Brian Wren, *What Language Shall I Borrow?* (London: SCM, 1989); also Julie Nelson, 'How I wept to hear your hymns', dissertation for MA in applied theology, College of St Mark and St John, Plymouth, 1995.

17 It is disturbing to note the evidence that 'surfing the Net' is increasingly popular among individuals with low social and relational skills, even as a substitute for genuine relating and community. The *Guardian* (8 April 1996) reported the popularity of games on the Internet among Japanese *men*, in which they create the girl-friend of their choice. This is seen as a reaction to the problem that Japanese *women* are dissatisfied with their traditional roles.

18 Of course, many members of AA and AlAnon are also members of churches, synagogues and mosques. But the shared interest which draws them together is not religious faith as such – even if this forms part of the journey to wholeness.

19 See Raghavan Iyer (ed.), *The Essential Writings of Mahatma Gandhi* (Delhi: Oxford University Press, 1990).

20 *Reconciliation: Gift of God and Source of New Life*, Study Guide for the Second European Ecumenical Assembly (London: CCBI Publications, 1995).

21 See Conrad Raiser, *Ecumenism in Transition* (Geneva: WCC, 1991).

22 Stanley Hauerwas, *After Christendom? How the Church Is to Behave If Freedom, Justice, and a Christian Nation Are Bad Ideas* (Nashville: Abingdon, 1991), p. 151, citing Lesslie Newbigin, *Foolishness to the Greeks: The Gospel in Western Culture* (Grand Rapids: Eerdmans, 1989), p. 115.

23 Ruether, *Women-Church*, p. 72.

24 Karl Rahner, 'Frommigkeit früher und heute' in *Schriften zur Theologie* VII (Einsiedeln, Zurich and Cologne, 1996), pp. 11–31.

25 This statement is made cautiously as (1) it has not been overcome in certain areas and we witness its savage aftermath, in particular, in places like East Timor: (2) new forms of colonialism and slavery, especially in the horrendous Third World debt problem, have arisen.

26 Hans Küng, *The Church*, tr. Ray and Rosaleen Ockenden (London and Tunbridge Wells: Search Press, 1968), pp. 358–9.

3

A CHRIST WHO 'GATHERS THE FRAGMENTS'?

Fragmentation, loss of soul and the absence of a common language have brought us to the brink, yet cannot be the end of the story. To recognize the Dark Night as a place of hanging on when hope is almost vanished and well-tried solutions have failed is itself a sign of hope. This is the place where, at last, we tell the truth to each other because a culture of deceit and lies has produced a diet of despair. Yet there is still a deeply rooted anxiety that *we may not know how to tell the truth to each other – at least publicly and institutionally.* As the Russian poet Irina Ratushinskaya sadly remarked, after the fall of communism in 1989,

> I have no values other than to tell no lies.[1]

But truth-telling is exactly what religion is about and the reason why it is at the level of ultimate truth, ultimate mystery, that solutions are to be *sought* – even if we actually *settle* for less. If fragmentation is the problem, *gathering the fragments* must be part of the process of redemption and healing; if loss of soul means that we live to trivialities and cheap values, then *recovery of soul* is part of the answer; if the loss of a common language is the problem, then communicating, encountering and hearing one another's truth is the solution.

This can only be done in full awareness of the culture of postmodernism: even if this is a term with an elusive character, defined in many different ways, it is a useful tool for understanding the shifting currents which influence culture. It is a term which evokes cultural diversity, resistance to universal solutions and raises political, economic and linguistic questions. At this moment, it is more the *climate* of postmodernism – rather than a particular expression of it – which keeps raising challenges to the post-Enlightenment rationalistic culture and to the political and technological hegemony of Euro-American societies. With great discernment Mark Kline Taylor in his book *Remembering Esperanza: A Cultural-Political Theology of North American Praxis* identified three dimensions of a postmodern culture which need a theological response and which I take as crucial for rethinking Church.[2] These – which he calls a postmodern trilemma – are *a sense of tradition, the celebration of plurality, and resistance to domination*. They are not themselves constitutive of a theology of Church: rather, as horns of a postmodern trilemma, they provide handles on our culture, which could prompt the Church's response. Conversely, failure to provide a response threatens religious communities with irrelevance at the very least.

Tradition, or traditioning as I will call it (all three dimensions are developed in Part Two), respects the heritage of the past. It simply asserts that the intermeshing communities (of place, race, faith) to which we belong have reached and maintain their identities through loyalties to what has been given and cherished by forerunners. But taken in conjunction with the other two dimensions (*celebrate plurality, resist domination*), traditioning highlights other facets than merely the observance of national days, or the coronation/inauguration of queen/president. The recognition of diversity brings the necessity of respecting and honouring smaller groups within a state – in a publicly recognized way. It calls attention to the fact that *Christian* holidays by and large dictate the calendar and bank holidays: what passes for multi-culturalism in churches and schools has only been a minimal response to the urgency for justice among culturally diverse groups. Hence the third horn of the dilemma is needed – *resist domination*. Whatever forms of domination are included within the definition – and Taylor includes sexism, hetero-sexism, racism and classism – *resisting domination* is closely linked with *celebrating pluralism* and *respecting tradition*. In fact one way of resisting domination may be achieved by honouring the traditions of culturally diverse groups and by seeing difference as strength, not as nuisance.

But to respond to diversity, tradition and struggle against oppression, it is particularly vital that the *Christian* Church knows its identity, and roots itself in an understanding of Christ rich enough to respond to this trilemma. It needs to ask, first, whether discipleship of Jesus of Nazareth can be recognized not merely as the following of a unique individual in the first century of the common era, but as an identifying quality of redemptive and grace-filled *Christic* community; second, whether this following today can respond in a transformative way to the dilemmas of culture. Specifically, what form of the following of Christ can respond to fragmentation by 'gathering the fragments' in an authentically redemptive manner?

Who are you, Christ, today? Where is your discipleship to be found?[3]

The poignant vignette of Christian community from Zeffirelli's film about Francis of Assisi, referred to in the last chapter, left us in no doubt that in the delightfully warm, informal eucharistic gathering around Francis and Clare, according to Franco Zeffirelli, *is authentic Christian community*. The tension we face in the churches between empty formalism and inclusive, involving styles of worship can seem unsurmountable. The participatory styles of being Church which followed the Second Vatican Council (to some extent) were a response to the fact that many people found the ceremonial formalism of traditional (male, hierarchical) worship alienating.

The question is even more challenging for a secular age: if the Church is experienced by many as alienating and corrupt, why not live out the Christian ideals – love of neighbour, forgiveness and moral decency, to which there is still a notional commitment in society – without belonging to the Christian Church at all? Clearly this is an option which has appealed to many young people. It could be described as *message Christology*. Accept – not Jesus but – his message. Further, the argument runs, since society is multi-cultural and largely secular, so without the embarrassment of Church membership or the legacy of Christian imperialism, we are more likely to achieve a tolerant coexistence with respect to widely divergent groups. Indeed, for Western Christians it might be a way of repenting from thrusting Christianity down the throats of Jews, Muslims and indigenous peoples throughout the history of Christendom! And what a relief not to have to justify the wealth of the Vatican in the face of the grinding poverty of many of Peter's obedient servants! The prophetic, icono-clastic figure of Jesus of Nazareth, our suffering brother in struggles for justice, who broke taboos in talking to women and despised groups of people – he is not our problem: but the institutional Church may be!

Undoubtedly this line of arguing has a certain force. When Mahatma Gandhi took the *message* of the Sermon on the Mount as foundational for his policy of non-violence, he neither became a disciple of Jesus, nor joined a Church. Indeed, he was convinced that Christianity had not even been tried. *Message Christology* is also in vogue with an assortment of groups which include feminist theologians (who see it as a solution to the maleness of Jesus), interfaith religious leaders (who see it as a solution to the unique claims of Jesus as universal saviour), and more secular figures – like the late Dag Hammarskjöld – who see the inspiration of Jesus as a way to transform political life.

Furthermore, since, as I have been arguing, it seems that the ethos of individualism has largely won, in a culture where privatization encroaches daily on the fabric of public life, it is small wonder that the *private following of Jesus,* or the assumption of *parts of his message* which happen to order personal behaviour without challenging public morality or inspiring social justice, are winning the day. A strand of Christian tradition appears to support this. From time to time there has been a reaction to a form of Christianity which tried to control public life excessively, expressing itself for example, in the form of Moravian Pietism[4] and Quietism,[5] both of which focused on the hidden life of prayer and the cultivation of the interior life. This individualistic following of Jesus can also be linked with what is perceived as the failure of liberation theology in certain parts of the world, for example, in post-Sandinista Nicaragua. When the search for the God of justice through the transformation of political and social structures appears to have failed, there is an abundance of evangelistic groups to persuade the disenchanted to follow the 'inner' message of Jesus.

A more nuanced attitude to 'traditioning' and to message Christology is needed. Clearly, the many groups who establish creative space on the periphery have developed a different response. Groups of 'loosely committed Christians' who exist without formal relationship to the established Church have developed another. Both of these categories are committed to the notion of *community* as the heart of the following of Jesus. As has been said, *the thirst for koinonia is not quenched* ... So the issue here is both whether authentic following of Jesus can happen without community, and whether this community necessarily must be an identifiable form of Christian Church.[6] If, as I have argued, where there is authentic following of Christ, there is Church, the question is how profoundly the core of this following is identifiable as *the prophetic stance of creative boundary living.* Will its authenticity be destroyed if its prophetic stance is not respected?

In the beginning, the relation ...

The inescapable feature about the earthly Jesus is not only that he brought close a God whose very being is relational – which is the core of the Christian doctrine of Trinity – but that he revealed the path to healing, redemption and transformation as consisting in right and just relationship. In fact he called people out of their isolation and alienated patterns of relating into a transformed relational way of being, where just relationships were the *embodiment of the dream of the Kingdom of God.* As Carter Heyward put it poetically: 'In the beginning was the relation and in the relation is the power that creates the world, through us, and with us, and by us, you and I, you and we, and none of us alone.'[7]

What that means in a context of individualism is that Christian discipleship offers a life-style completely opposed to the privatized, consumerist ethic, exploitative both of the planet's resources and of groups of poor people whom it considers expendable. For Jesus revealed sin as *separation*:[8] not only the construction of barriers between rich and poor, and the structural deafness which refuses to let in a different truth from the dominant story, but a *blocking off from the patterns which connect body and spirit, humanity and nature*. It is striking that *binding images* are at the heart of his parables: 'To what shall I compare the kingdom of God? It is like leaven which a woman took and hid in three measures of meal, till it was all leavened' (Luke 13:20). It is the *yeast of right and just relation* which is the stuff of the Kingdom of God, whereas (in my opinion) it is the yeast of Herod, against which the disciples are warned, which is the *yeast of separation*. But it is not only yeast which is the image of the binding agent of the Kingdom: Jesus himself functions as this, for 'Where two or three are gathered, in my name, there am I in the midst of them' (Matthew 18:20).

What is fundamental to the understanding of the Kingdom of God is, first, that we cannot approach Jesus except within this great dream and project – since he himself situated all his teaching in this context – and, second, this relational reality is only understood as a *broken body* which somehow incorporates the broken and persecuted peoples of the world: 'A body broken for a broken people' was how Francis Moloney described the core meaning of the eucharist.[9] This is the only way we can make sense of Paul's stress on the Body of Christ – Paul, who seems not to know much about, or at least does not make central to his teaching, the person of the earthly Jesus. Hence the extraordinary identification of the persecuted early Christians with the body of the suffering Jesus, with and for whom they suffered. Both women and men identified with this suffering Christ. A poignant example of this is the story of Perpetua and Felicitas who, with a small community of Christians in third-century Carthage, were thrown to the lions in the arena. When Felicitas, forced to give birth to her baby in prison, was taunted by the gaoler: ' "If you're complaining now, what will you do when you're thrown to the wild beasts?" She answered: "Now it is I who suffer, but then another shall be in me, since I am now suffering for him ... " '[10] This moving story takes us to the core of the meaning of Christian discipleship: that *Christic community itself – in its prophetic, resisting action – is the constitutive heart of who Christ is.*

Contemporary debates have focused on whether the male gender of Jesus determines the question of who can represent him, and what degree of significance this has for the incarnation and the question of women's ordination.

Yet Christologies from different parts of the world are revealing a much greater fluidity as to the gender of Jesus. Yes, Jesus was male; but he was man in such a way as to be capable of being represented as a woman. *Celebrating pluralism* in Christology itself reveals a relational Christ, an ecological Christ, calling diverse and suffering communities to new expressions of power-in-relationship. Hence also *resisting domination*. What the story of Felicitas says is that it is the identification of Christ with the suffering and broken people – and vice versa – which is the hallmark of discipleship, because this is how healing and transformative energy is generated. Yes, Jesus is mediator of relational power – *but in direct relation to the Messianic communities where it is generated.*

For to be a saviour figure is not to be a conventional hero like Robin Hood or El Cid. If it was, then there would be no contradiction in having our privatized posters of the hero Jesus, with whom we communicate individually. Jesus is rather *anti-hero*, turning the hero-concept on its head. He showed, instead, that redemptive power works relationally. As the earthly Jesus, he empowered people as agents in their own self-becoming (for example Zacchaeus, the woman with the issue of blood, the Syro-Phoenician woman): through Jesus they were able to lay claim to their own relational strengths. Even in the most desperate of circumstances there are possibilities for relating. To remain vulnerable to this possibility – and not to give way to a destructive isolation or self-absorption – is to be open to divine redemptive action. Christ – in an extraordinary openness to a diversity of relations, both teaching and being taught – showed that the roots of the healing process must be grounded in the material and social realities of the whole of life. *Matter matters* is the message. Not for nothing does the Christology developed by Mark Kline Taylor (later in *Remembering Esperanza*) take as starting point the image of *Christus Mater*: focusing on the material realities of poor women as mothers as entry-point to a new Christology, he is able to see this Christ-figure as challenge and corrective to sexism, hetero-sexism, racism and economic poverty.[11]

It is a process being repeated globally through the discovery of the black Christ, the many Christa figures (including the bleeding Christa of Bosnia), the Christ of Asia who is nursing mother and shaman, tree of life, as well as suffering brother. If 'Where there is following of Christ, there is Church' – but not necessarily vice versa – is the yardstick, then, where there is genuine Messianic community open to and claiming the mutuality of power-in-relation, the community is making this vulnerable Christ present. And the surprisingly new dimension is that through these christological images *women are acknowledged as participating in the nexus of symbols which mediate sacred power.*

Where these examples of discipleship and Messianic communities are at their most vibrant, is, unsurprisingly, on the periphery, the prophetic margins, in 'creative boundary living'.[12] Yet, as long as these groups remain on the margins, their existence is tolerated. But the dilemma is that once the prophetic groups challenge the centre, the solid weight of institutional authority comes into play. The dilemma is that loyalty to the centre demands submission, yet loyalty to the prophetic core seeks another solution. It is precisely to discover a way out of the dilemma, true to the prophetic nature of Christ-community, yet offering a way forward to institutional Church, that so many loyal Christians find themselves wrestling with the Dark Night.

A new Church, waiting to be born?

Approaching the millennium, hopes and dreams abound. Millennial times are times when the prophetic Spirit of God is perceived as active. It can be cautiously admitted that there are signs that a quiet revolution is under way, that the seeds of renewal which the Church so desperately needs, if it is to be seen as authentic following of Jesus, responding to the contemporary threefold trilemma, are indeed at hand. Seven factors are pointing the way.

First, communal following of Christ presents a *counter-cultural challenge to the ethics of individualism and competitive materialism.* In this sense the social teaching of the Church ecumenically, and in particular, the more than a hundred years' tradition of political and social critique developed by the Roman Catholic magisterium, is an invaluable resource. There is no way that the individualized following of the hero Jesus (however inspirational) can have such a structural impact.

Where this communal following is now found at its most vibrant is both among poor people in the basic ecclesial communities with their powerful hunger for social justice, as well as in the growing evangelical groups whose emphasis is on prayer, fellowship and social action. This was the same hunger for a different culture called for by Rodolfo Cardenal (see Chapter 1), when he challenged the powerful nations to develop a culture of simplicity to enable the 'crucified peoples' of Central America to survive.

Third, from the plurality of Christologies now developing, the accent has shifted from the person of Jesus to *the redeeming dynamic which he sets in motion.* The contextualized needs of the community – hunger for justice, resistance to oppression, the need to come to terms with pluralism and the cherished traditions which have shaped the community – are all affecting the shape of emergent Christologies. This diversity in understanding Jesus today, instead of giving cause for concern, is rather fuelling the conviction that Christology can be transformative of culture (see Chapter 7).

Excessive concern for uniformity only serves to suppress the *redemptive potential of christological symbolism*. The burning need today is for understandings of Christ's uniqueness which will not obliterate but nurture understanding and sharing with other faith communities. Hence a further criterion for Christian discipleship will be recognized as the degree of openness to divine truth revealed across the religious traditions. Faith community engaging with faith community – this is both discipleship and prerequisite for world peace.

Yet another pointer issues from feminist theology's reflection on the ministry of women. Whether this springs from Anglican and Free Church experience of the actual praxis of women's ministry, or from Roman Catholic commitment to collaborative ministry, the force of the theological core which emerges cannot be suppressed. That women bring gifts to ministry born of commitment to mutuality, empathy and right relationship is part of this. That women seem to have a deep capacity for forgiveness for centuries of exclusion and discrimination is astonishing. But there is more to it. What Roman Catholic women are now saying, with a degree of urgency, is that the mere permission for the ordination of women will not solve deeply rooted ecclesial problems: *a radical re-think of discipleship and the nature of Church along prophetic and non-hierarchical lines is what is urgently needed*.[13] If discipleship is seen on communal/relational lines, then the community itself embodies and represents the suffering and risen faces of Jesus – and community consists of both women and men.

The fifth pointer is a counterbalance to a theology of structural sin. Sin has its structures – but *grace has its structures too*. Authentic following of Christ means that grace-filled encounters are enabled through the quality of community. Young people are exploring new expressions of Church and active discipleship within, for example, the ambience of creation spirituality, Iona, Corrymeela and Taizé communities – to give just a few European examples – as well as through Women-Church on a global scale. The Christology inspiring these examples is, first, the ecological Christ, as the pattern which connects the whole of creation – extending the idea of community beyond the merely human; the thirst for social justice in all its expressions, and the affirmation that women are church, and *Christa community* is where Messianic power is nurtured and shared.[14]

The next two points are closely linked. Millennial times are the age of the Spirit – the Spirit of Christ and of God. It is the role of the Spirit to discover the cracks of culture, open up new possibilities and to lead into a yet uncharted future – as will be explored in Part Three. It can be no accident that from various Christian communities the search for prophetic leadership is becoming powerful, a leadership which is shared, which enables and empowers the gifts of others. It is no accident that the Spirit is creating a new vulnerability towards listening and acknowledging the truth of others, particularly the truth of groups on the periphery – like people with AIDS and the gay community.

But how does the Spirit respond to culture's preference for privatized following of Jesus? By recognizing that social action is not enough, that people also hunger to experience God in the depth of their hearts, the dimensions of mysticism and contemplation are being rediscovered, not as the private possession of the élite, but as the rootedness of the entire People of God in the presence of Christ. This is a presence which binds, heals and connects with the life-renewing energies of the cosmos itself.

This expression – prophetic and mystical – of the communal discipleship of Jesus which is suggestive of a renewed Church is well expressed by the inspiring words of the late Penny Lernoux, a journalist in Latin America:

> The People of God will continue their march, despite the power plays and intrigue in Rome. And the Third World will continue to beckon to the west, reminding it of the Galilean vision of solidarity. As a young Guatemalan said, a few months before she was killed by the military, 'What good is life unless you give it away – unless you can give it for a better world, even if you never see that world but have only carried your grain of sand to the building site. Then you're fulfilled as a person.'[15]

Fulfilment, self-realization, yes: but only Christian if in the solidarity of prophetic community which has the courage to persevere in existence on the boundaries.

Perhaps a profound Jewish idea will move us forward. What I have described as culture's fragmentation, the shattered foundations of culture, is expressed by the Kabbalistic story of sin, expressed by the broken fragments of creation. Redemption, conversely, is seen as *gathering the fragments*, as *tikkun olam*,[16] the process of mending and healing, of creating whatever wholeness is possible. God's work – but the work too of all Messianic communities, committed to witness through prophetic and creative boundary living.

Notes

1 Irina Ratushinskaya, cited by Dominic Kirkham, 'A new European awakening', *The Month* (November 1991), p. 471.

2 Mark Kline Taylor, *Remembering Esperanza: A Cultural-Political Theology of North American*

Praxis (Maryknoll: Orbis, 1990), ch. 1.

3 Some of the material which follows has been adapted from my article 'Jesus, guru of individualism or community's heart?', *Concilium* (1997/1), pp. 120–8.

4 Continental Pietism was a movement greatly renewing Protestant life in the seventeenth and eighteenth centuries. A reaction partly to moral lassitude, and partly to clergy control, it encouraged people to discover their own spiritual priesthood through conversion, prayerful Bible study and devotions: *Dictionary of Spirituality*, ed. Cheslyn Jones et al. (London: SPCK, 1986), pp. 448–53.

5 Quietism was a seventeenth-century movement usually associated with Mme Guyon and Fénelon, Archbishop of Cambrai. Mme Guyon stressed the union of the soul with God coupled with detachment from the world: ibid., pp. 408–15.

6 When Charles Davis left the priesthood in 1967 he took the option of being Christian without explicit commitment to a particular church. But it is difficult to find a group which has stood the test of time.

7 Carter Heyward, *The Redemption of God: A Theology of Mutual Relation* (Washington, DC: University of America Press, 1980), p. 172. The theme 'In the beginning is the relation' is of course from Martin Buber, *I and Thou* (Edinburgh: T. & T. Clark, 1958), p. 18.

8 See M. Grey, *The Wisdom of Fools?* (London: SPCK, 1993), ch. 5, 'The separate self and the denial of relation'.

9 Francis Moloney, *A Body Broken for a Broken People* (Melbourne: Collins Dove, 1990).

10 P. Wilson Kastner, G. R. Kastner et al. (eds), 'The martyrdom of Perpetua: a protest account of early Christianity' in *A Lost Tradition: Women Writers of the Early Church* (Washington, DC: University Press of America, 1981), p. 27.

11 See Mark Kline Taylor, op. cit., ch. 6, 'Christus Mater'.

12 See Hannah Ward and Jennifer Wild, *Guard the Chaos: Finding Meaning in Change* (London: Darton, Longman and Todd, 1995).

13 See Elisabeth Schüssler Fiorenza, lecture 'Feminist women-priests – an oxymoron?', World Ordination Conference, 1995.

14 For the idea of Christa community, see Rita Nakashima Brock, *Journeys by Heart: A Christology of Erotic Power* (New York: Crossroad, 1988).

15 Penny Lernoux, cited in Jim Wallis, *Soul of Politics* (San Diego and New York: Harcourt Brace and Co., Harvester, 1995), p. 252.

16 The word *tikkun* belongs especially to Jewish Kabbalistic mysticism and is associated with the sixteenth-century writer Isaac Luria. *Tikkun olam* means 'cosmic repair': 'For the mystic, deeds of *tikkun* (cosmic repair) sustain the worth, activate nature to praise God ... Related to the contraction of God, the breaking of the vessels and the exiled sparks, was Luria's conception of *tikkun*. For Lurianic mystics, this concept refers to the mending of what was broken during the shattering of vessels. After the catastrophe in the divine realm, the process of restoration began and every disaster was seen as a setback in this process. In this battle, keeping God's commandments was understood as contributing to repair – the divine sparks which fell down can be redeemed by ethical and religious deed ... When the process is complete evil will disappear, but every time a Jew sins a spark is captured and plunges into the satanic abyss': Dan Cohn-Sherbok, *The Jewish Faith* (London: SPCK, 1993), pp. 73, 74–5.

PART TWO

IN SEARCH OF THE BELOVED COMMUNITY

Stay well connected to our embodied selves and question the dualism of those who try to separate us from our own bodies and from our own kitchen table realities. Stay well connected *to your communities of faith and struggle* and question those who use dogma to prevent spiritual gifts of transformation from being shared at the round table. Stay connected as well *to the margins* and question those who perpetuate contradictions and structures of domination that deny the hospitality of God's welcome table to the 'outsiders'. For those who wish to open themselves and their churches to what new thing God might be doing in their lives, I can only say 'Stay well-connected' and perhaps you will discover the gift of church in the round in and through the many table connections that disturb and nourish us day by day.

Letty Russell, *Church in the Round* (Louisville, KY: Westminster John Knox, 1993), p. 206.

4

JOURNEYING

Journeying as dimension of becoming Church needs neither explanation nor justification. The pilgrim people of God journeying through the desert, searching for a Promised Land, has long been a guiding image for us.[1] The Russian *strannik* or pilgrim revered in the culture of Russian Orthodoxy has acquired fresh importance through Catherine de Hueck Doherty's spirituality of contemplation in a busy urban life.[2] Indeed, there must be scarcely an ancient culture in which journeying to the holy man – or woman (the priestess of the god Pythian Apollo played an important part in Greek history) – has not been significant. From Russia, too, comes the story of the Babushka's pilgrimage. On an icy wintry night, so the story goes, on the Eve of Epiphany, the three Wise Men knocked on the door of the Babushka's cottage and invited her to journey with them to Bethlehem to find the newborn Prince of Peace. But Babushka was old, the night was dark and stormy, the snow was deep, and Babushka was afraid. So they journeyed on alone. But the next day she set out to visit all the poor children around the countryside, bringing them gifts. She would never reach Bethlehem: but the words of the Wise Men ring deep in her heart: 'Further on, Babushka, further on . . .'[3] What is this, but the archetypal quality of the call to keep searching?

The medieval idea of pilgrimage as atonement for sin had a deep grasp on both popular practice and imagination. No one who has read the Norwegian writer Sigrid Undset's three-volume saga of *Kristin Lavransdatter* could fail to have been gripped by Kristin's pilgrimage over the mountains, her baby on her back, carrying a little bread and salt, in atonement for the sin of conceiving a child before marriage:

> The grass was as a grey fur coverlid with the heavy dew, as Kristin walked to the church; but the sunlight was golden on the woods that topped the ridge, and the cuckoo called from the hillside – it looked as though she would have fair weather for her pilgrimage.
>
> There was none in the choir save Erlend [her husband] and his wife, and the

two priests in the lighted choir. Erlend looked across at Kristin's naked feet. Ice-cold it must be for her, standing on the stone floor. She was to walk the twenty miles with no other company than their prayers. He strove to lift up his heart to God, so as he had not striven for many years.

She was clad in an ashen-grey kirtle, and had a rope about her waist. Underneath, he knew, she wore a shift of sackcloth. A tightly bound wadmal cloth hid her hair.[4]

In a saga in which the predominant theme is atonement for a sin which haunts the entire work, without a counterbalance in a history of grace and forgiveness, the element which grips here is the importance of this atoning (and punitive?) pilgrimage for the essence of Church. *There is nothing private about Kristin's journey.*

But the vital element is to discover if the *matrix of symbols* which encapsulate the many motives for pilgrimage can be re-contextualized as a springboard for a new theology of Church.

First, it is striking that journeying as pilgrimage has taken on a new lease of life, culturally speaking. The journey to Jerusalem, the pilgrimage to Mecca, will always be deeply significant to Jewish and Muslim communities. But there is a new growth in the activity of pilgrimage wider than the official faith communities. It would be cynical to dismiss this purely as a consequence of people having more leisure and money to travel: pilgrim people span the generations and economic classes. There is something strikingly counter-cultural in pilgrimages of the sick to Lourdes, of young people with back-packs climbing the mountain to Taizé, or walking the dusty road to Chartres, or barefoot up the mountain of Croagh Patrick, at a time when the cross-channel ferries have been metamorphosed into palaces of pleasure, air-flights into gourmet experiences and when railways speak of customers instead of pas-sengers. Could pilgrimage in its simplicity, discipline of prayer and shared ideals be one sign that culture has not completely lost soul? Of course the resurgence of Celtic spirituality has highlighted the distinctly Celtic *peregrinatio* (wandering): it has sparked off the idea of journeying with a common ideal to both Christian and pre-Christian sites. Pilgrimages for peace are undertaken both to ancient sacred places and to more contemporary shrines as peoples of all faiths unite, in the hope that their solidarity forges peace and justice in a local context. Pilgrimages to holy wells, mountains and ancient groves take on a contextual meaning of protection of the environment. This contemporary search or quest for the sacred of course evokes the ancient quest for the holy Grail with echoes in many epochs and civilizations. It has a particularly poignant significance in challenging us to ask new questions and to articulate what is sacred today.[5] Even the journeying itself – and the telling of stories along the way – acquires a new meaning in a postmodern culture. Simply to be journeying, asking questions, suggests a challenging of old certainties, a seeking of new connections. It is evoking both a new search for silence, for contemplation, a discovery of – and a hanging on to – a centred stillness[6] as well as an attempt to gather the fragmented insights which occur on the journey into another coherence: this itself will nurture further searching. James Hillman names this wandering search the 'errant way'.

> The errant way leads to the less well-known for sure, to less knowledge as established, as accumulated into security . . . The psychological mirror that walks down the road, the Knight Errant on his adventure, the scrounging rogue is also an odd-job man, like *Eros the Carpenter* [my italics] who joins this bit with that.[7]

This delightful image of Eros the Carpenter I take as inspirational both for the *desire* which stimulates and sustains the quest, and the *hope* it brings of reconfiguring the fragmentation according to a different pattern.

But it is the quest, not merely of individuals, but at the heart of faith communities which draws on the *condensed* symbolism of exodus from oppression, wandering in the wilderness – while experiencing the presence of God in a new way – and hoping for the Promised Land. It is this condensed symbolism which asks for re-contextualization. For it is not at all clear that liberation theology's original inspiration of exodus from oppression and hope for the justice of the Promised Land continues to provide the dynamism for further movement. Three examples illustrate this. At the Assembly of the Ecumenical Forum of European Christian Women (EFECW) in 1990, delegates were moved by a mime presented by Eastern European women. They presented themselves as wandering in the desert, but without the vision of the Promised Land to energize them. These were women from the 'newly liberated' communist countries: the vision of the socialist Utopia had vanished, and what remained were the seductive arms of capitalism. *Wandering in the wilderness without vision* summed up their situation symbolically.

The second example is from post-Sandinista Nicaragua.[8] The euphoria of the Sandinista revolution had seemed to usher in the glimpses of the Promised Land, as the country began to recover from the terrorism of the Contras and the Somoza regime. But how does this symbolism now work, in the wake of the tragic defeat of the Sandinistas in the elections of 1990? It seems to some liberation theologians that the memory of the Babylonian captivity would more aptly symbolize the shock of loss of hope and the experience of being in captivity to the capitalist systems.[9] Even the Beast of Revelation has an obvious focus – seen as domination by market forces.

The same symbolic nexus fits the third example, which is the racist discrimination experienced by numerous ethnic groups, not to mention asylum-seekers. To speak of 'exodus from oppression' could now be counter-productive. Even if the heritage of negro spirituals is a precious one, keeping alive the dangerous memory of suffering and slavery and the dream of a better world than this one, black communities in Europe and America need a symbolism of *rightful belonging and citizenship*. The mixed messages of the Babylon captivity go some way towards this. But better still is the symbolism of *from Babel to Pentecost* and the movement from one to the other.[10] Babel – symbol of racial confusion and pride – gives way, through the energizing of the Spirit, to racial diversity experienced as gift, harmony and enrichment.

Furthermore, the message of this book is *not* that we should exodus from institutional Church. It is true that this has become a popular option. The dramatic call of Mary Daly has been answered by many who can no longer sustain the pain of what the Church has become. Daphne Hampson describes the impact:

> I remember as though it were yesterday standing in the kitchen of Episcopal Theological School in Cambridge, Massachusetts, when my friend Diane burst in to tell me the news. It must have been November 1971. She had been at the morning service in Harvard Yard and one Mary Daly – of whom I had never heard – had delivered a sermon inviting women to exodus from the church – and women and men had poured into Harvard Yard. History had been made; and I had been absent! Diane became a priest. Mary Daly left the Church. I myself at that time could not have conceived of leaving the church and Christianity behind me. For twenty years I wanted to be ordained. But I have left.[11]

There is, of course, a well-established meaning to exodus, as *exodus from alienated relationship*, as Daphne Hampson describes it in the same article:

> Exodus can mean literally leaving, going out into a new existence. Over the years, since the rise of feminism innumerable women have walked out on marriages in which they were being abused, jobs in which they were discriminated against, or the church in which they were unable to be ordained.[12]

It can also mean, she continues, a kind of internal exodus, a being absent mentally, while present physically, within structures which alienate. But when Rosemary Ruether called for an exodus, she did not mean a literal exodus from institutional Church. Rather,

> We call on our brothers to join us in exodus from the land of patriarchy, to join

49

us in our common quest for that promised land where there will be no more war, no more burning children, no more discarded elderly, no more rape of the earth.[13]

So it is this exodus from alienated relationships within the Church which I take as the leitmotiv of today's journey. All hierarchical dualisms (whether man/woman, humanity/animal, body/soul, nature/culture, clerical/lay) belong to this category, says Ruether. A sacramental life which alienates large categories of believers from the table of the eucharist is in danger of being *alienated sacramental life*. For the eucharist, as Francis Moloney writes in *A Body Broken for a Broken People* (cited in Chapter 3), originates not only as a commemoration of Jesus' Last Supper, but from all the meals he shared with sinners, tax-collectors, prostitutes, the broken-hearted, the lame and the handicapped.[14] A theology of sexuality which condemns to the status of deviants — and creates another category of outcasts — a large proportion of human beings, is *alienated sexuality*. Understandings of power, priesthood and authority which reduce the pilgrim people to disempowerment and passivity are *alienated understandings*.

Furthermore, ecumenical and interfaith movements are at a particularly sensitive moment in history. To be on a journey need not mean that we should all alter our loyalties and change churches, however green the grass may seem on the other side. (This is not for a moment to challenge the faith journey of those who have taken this step: the discernment needed and pain which this has caused can never be fathomed by outsiders.) Yet, despite the errant antics of Eros the Carpenter (see above), it does not mean that there is no value in standing firm. It could be that this *kairos* calls for creative boundary living and prophetic action right here, in our own patch of ground.

The inclination of many women is in fact to stay, not to go! *Women are not quitters!* (Elisabeth Schüssler Fiorenza rejected 'exodus' as symbol for Women-Church for this very reason.) Women stay and remake the situation from whatever resources they can tap. A story told by Eva Vörös, a minister from the Hungarian Reformed Church, from the recent war in the former Yugoslavia, illustrates this poignantly:

> Maria is a minister's wife, ethnic Hungarian, yet living in Vojvodina, Serbian territory, through all the horrors of ethnic cleansing. And for these ethnic Hungarians, the very real fear is always that they are next on the list — and many have already been killed by the Serbs. Some months ago when hundreds of young men received a call for military service in the Serbian army, the women organized a protest — which was actually successful. But even since then 300 men have been forced to leave her village — probably for refugee camps.[15]

The point I am making is that here, in a context of war, it is to the women, and in this case Maria, that it falls to create and maintain any sense of faith and hope in Christian community. Her own faith had been tested when she had been saved through prayer from rape by Russian and Serbian soldiers. She and her husband, though reduced to poverty and unable to offer their former hospitality, yet are loyal to a vision of Christianity which is in *exodus from the current situation*. In fact, he is deliberately endangering his own life by choosing texts on peace and preaching, even though this is seen as flagrantly opposing the Serbian government.

Maria, courageously sustaining community in a war situation, calls to mind another Miriam: Carol Ochs, in a recent article, creatively depicts in a midrashic way the ministry of the biblical Miriam in war situations. While Moses, leader on the journey, publicly exhorts the people, Miriam is creating community in the wilderness, binding the wounds, leading liturgies which encourage and comfort:

> The men were left without anything when Moses ascended Sinai. They had been taken out of their former roles as slaves, but now Moses, who had given them their vision of freedom, had disappeared in the cloud on the mountain and they were left without guidance. The women, meanwhile, returned to their tents, and Miriam was telling them that in their tasks and their chores they would experience revelation.
>
> Through these tasks and chores they had created worlds – of feeding their families, of caring for their children – and these worlds sustained them. They did not even understand the meaning of either the men's panic or their own steadiness; least of all did they grasp how their daily work was related to revelation. Only as Miriam spoke with them, one by one, did they begin to see that the very future of the Israelites was at stake. When Moses returned and smashed the Tablets of the Law, and three thousand were put to the sword that day, the women comforted the living, tended the orphans, and mourned, while nursing those who suffered from the plague. All the while, Miriam reminded the women that *this* was revelation: birth and family, dailiness and death.[16]

Though it may be confusing to divide ministry in gender-stereotypic ways, yet creative imagination is a key tool in journeying from alienated forms of Christian living – as will be explored in Chapter 8: Miriam, a forgotten prophetic woman from the very roots of the Jewish exodus tradition, is a precious resource in journeying for Jewish, Christian and Islamic faith communities alike.

But another way forward is to make creative use of mythic material *outside* Jewish and Christian traditions to stimulate us out of trapped patterns of thinking. So to make that step forward, another journey is explored here: *the journey of Psyche to find Eros*. It is explored in order to make the links to the *search for soul* in contemporary society (see Part One), and to show that in order for Christian community to discover more meaningful patterns of relating beyond destructive dualisms, rethinking our own humanity in the specificity of cultural understandings must be courageously tackled. Why the journey of Psyche and Eros? *Because Psyche's journey is a journey to acquire 'face'.*

Till We Have Faces, as many will be aware, is the title of a book by C. S. Lewis, where he retells the old Romano-Greek myth of Psyche and Eros.[17] This, one of the founding myths of European culture – with roots in Indian myth – is the story of the King and Queen who, on the instructions of the god Apollo, abandoned their beautiful daughter Psyche – of whom Aphrodite was jealous – on a mountain top. Then Eros, Aphrodite's son – he of the playful arrows – fell in love with her and had the west wind carry her off to a palace. Their happiness together is ruined when Psyche disobeys instructions and looks on his face when he is asleep. Eros flees, betrayed, and Psyche, pregnant, searching for him, must undergo some terrible tasks, which are a kind of female equivalent of the Labours of Hercules. After completion of the worst of these, a descent to the underworld to obtain Persephone's ointment, they are reunited, both transformed.

So why this journey into mythic imagination, after what seemed like a straightforward discussion of the meaning and re-contextualizing of biblical exodus as foundational symbol? After all, Lewis's retelling of the story held no direct political or theological message – although it had plenty of cultural and educational spin-offs.

First, to look into the most influential myths which form our basic ideas of integrity, trust, longing, relationship and the sacred may yield valuable insights. In Christianity, Judaism and Islam, the Adamic myth – Adam, Eve, the serpent and expulsion from Paradise – is acknowledged to underpin many cultural attitudes and the psychic imagination, not to mention our moral behaviour. The sense of being fallen, guilty, of being expelled from the garden, with an irretrievable lost innocence, of women's supposed greater responsibility for sin and moral behaviour – I think of the title of the barrister Helena Kennedy's book, *Eve Was Framed!*[18] – is so deeply embedded in our consciousness that we may be no longer aware that parts of this legacy inhibit growth to maturity and relationship (relationship understood on both personal and structural levels).[19] So two factors justify this calling on a Greek myth to provide a new entry point. Our philosophic mindset has no qualms in recognizing that Christianity built upon the great constructions of Plato and Aristotle. Be it theology, philosophy or politics, the ideas of the Greeks are still a jumping-off point. But the philosopher Martha Nussbaum, in her book *The Fragility of Goodness*,[20] points out that the human situation is so fraught with tragedy and ambiguity that we need to pay greater attention not just to the philosophers, but also to the way Greek tragedy has depicted this in all its starkness.

Second, the linguistic philosopher and psychoanalyst Julia Kristeva pointed out that feminism came to birth at a time when there was a crisis about culture's understanding of the nature of love. She speaks of women's refusal to accept an identity based on insertion into a social structure, or a symbolic order, as she puts it, *which was sacrificial to female identity.*[21] There must be a new ethics, a 'Her-ethics' of the second sex, to express what she calls *jouissance*, the laughing/playful/creative and affective dimension of female sexuality. In other words, a new language for loving. So *Till We Have Faces* acts as a metaphor for the search for a new, reconfigured identity for both men and women, and for *lost or hidden dimensions of the personality to acquire visibility*. It is, in fact, a story of soul-making for a culture which has lost its soul.

I am suggesting that looking at the myth of Psyche and Eros could offer one way out of some of the cultural and religious impasses which civilization in the northern hemisphere faces. A few years ago, beginning to look at this, I was amazed by the energy which different groups of people have invested in the story. First, it is now frequently used as a feminist myth of redemption in circles of spirituality and psychoanalysis.[22] Psyche is seen as a woman in search of identity and maturity and is helped by the natural world in the accomplishment of all her tasks, which are of an initiatory character. Eros, too, is transformed from being the little boy who will not grow up – a kind of Greek Peter Pan – into someone who learns to take responsibility for loving. Aphrodite is revealed for what she really is – a patriarchal construct. C. S. Lewis dug deep imaginatively to find the old Earth Mother figure underneath the newer jealous figure she became in later mythology and in the Christianized versions of the earlier traditions.[23]

Second, Psyche and Eros are beloved of psychologists and psychoanalysis. The work of James Hillman, for example, has used the myth to re-imagine and re-envision psychology not as an individualistic discipline, but as a revitalization of culture as a whole. Third, there is a theological and educational challenge in using the myth as critique of the value systems of individualist consumerism. For the myth of Psyche and Eros shows how Europe is 'split at the roots', particularly in its conceptualizing of love.[24] This dualistic splitting which grips European consciousness, right across the span of religions and those with no religious adherence, is clear in the polarizing of the pernicious dualisms already referred to. As was discovered in Chapter 2's search for a common understanding of Church, there *is* 'no shared language' – Adrienne Rich's *Dream of a Common Language*.

But it is a dilemma on a more crucial level. At a political level the only universally accepted language is that of human rights. Even there we do not agree: do animals have them or not? Should only the intelligent animals have them? Does the earth have any rights? Does the command to love yourself and your neighbour include animals and non-sentient beings? Are we commanded to love the rain-forest?

Many contemporary theologians who work towards an embodied theology are trying so hard to overcome this splitting-at-the-roots, to achieve a holistic language, an *embodied* spirituality, *embodied* humanity, that they have lost touch with 'soul talk'. Chapter 2 introduced Etty Hillesum's attempts to create a landscape for the soul in the context of 'gathering the fragments'. Calling on mythic resources at this point reinforces the point that *Psyche* language is *soul* language. It was sadly evident in all the discussions in 1992 on 'the New Europe' that there were no ideals and values beyond the narrowly economic being built into the construction of the new Europe. If Europe is seen purely as a trading club, its constituent members vying for the best deal they can get, weakly motivated for wider responsibilities, then there is no collective soul language with which to challenge the value system. The blame should not only be put on secularism, but more on the fact that, at a very deep level, our understanding of *psyche*/soul has shrunk to an over-individualized plane. *There is a profound splitting at the roots*. For example, the language of 'free will' is understood in an individualistic way which polarizes the will against emotion and desire. Moral choices are seen as narrowly rational choices: it is either 'pro-life' or 'pro-choice', says the most famous example of this, as if there was no middle ground, no outcome respecting a wider moral scene. Even though the language of feeling has reappeared in therapy and counselling, the splitting-at-the-roots between desire/feeling and reason/logic, is not healed. *Eros and Psyche remain alienated*. Worse still, we live in times, says James Hillman, when our very understanding of Eros, desire, yearning, is debased, literally soulless, a *soulless eroticism*: But for Eros to find Psyche, he says, this individualistic splitting-at-the-roots has to be overturned. Hence he is convinced that 'Psyche and Eros' is a myth for our times: 'Eros and Psyche offer more than Oedipus. It speaks to our times when the need of the soul is for love and the need of *eros* is for *psyche*. We suffer and are ill from their separation.'[25] The sickness to which Hillman refers is not simply at the level of individuals, but a cultural, communal phenomenon. Our mythic imagination is dead, and, as I argued in

The Wisdom of Fools?, we live by the logos myth, which is individualistic, profit-centred, competitive, ruthless in valuing human and non-human life solely for its financial value to the economy.

Because Europe has not faced this challenge, has allowed Psyche to wander, homeless, a vagabond, yet suffering, and encouraged Eros to play his mindless, malicious, self-centred games, rejecting all responsibility, the most appalling forms of erotic satisfaction in society have been legitimated: child prostitution in India and mail-order brides from Thailand are just two examples. They are just two forms of exploitative neo-colonialism that many Third World women are forced into, to satisfy the unfulfilled *eros* of the northern hemisphere.[26] *They have no faces* – veiled, literally, but denied dignity at a basic human level.

The recent controversial film *Bandit Queen* tells the story of the Indian woman Phoolan Devi, kidnapped by bandits as a child, raped repeatedly, and forced into a life of banditry in the Chambal valley of Madya Pradesh. Eventually she was persuaded to surrender, imprisoned with all her gang and, after years of captivity, released. What her story says loud and clear is: *this is the end of the road*. This terrible mixture of violence, poverty, the hidden culture in the Chambal valley – a territory of ravines, desert, aridity, where banditry had flourished for hundreds of years and a kind of Robin Hood morality ruled the day – is where it ends, when *eros*, the fundamental creative power of loving, is so divorced from any form, purpose, dignity: that is, divorced *from psyche*.

'Till we have faces', then, is a metaphor begging that the selfhood of women be respected, and given new expression in the many symbols and images which express our cultural values.

The legend contains yet more promise. Catherine Keller points out that Psyche's real quest is motivated by *eros* – but because psyche/soul always refuses to love blindly, because she refuses to merge unconsciously in the night – in other words to surrender mindlessly – she is punished by the worst thing of all, separation. Psyche yearns for *intelligent loving* – and culture is obdurately split at the roots. Psyche will have Eros on new and equal terms. 'Love is blind', they say, but Psyche/Soul will love with open eyes, 'laying responsible claim to relatedness'.[27]

The question for a theology of Church is to discern how Christian theology has contributed to this process of the splitting at the roots. The clue lies, as I have indicated earlier, in Julia Kristeva's declaration that feminism entered culture because of a failure in the understanding of love. Christian tradition, buying into the damaging dualisms of Greek philosophy, has over-idealized suffering as a means to holiness. Pleasure and *eros* were tolerated within strictly defined conditions, but in the end *eros* must cede to *agape*, defined as a love which is totally other-centred. Add this to the Gospel command to 'lose your life in order to find it', and then there is a socially sanctified way to justify suffering and victimhood for the sake of the supposed sanctity to follow. Suffering in this vale of tears gains us our heavenly crown. The doctrine of the Atonement itself – in many interpretations – is frequently interpreted as encouraging an ethic of self-sacrifice and expiation. In imitating the sacrifice of Christ, the oblation of the Beloved Son to satisfy the honour of the Father, a rigid foundation is encountered on which this splitting at the roots is built. Psyche and Eros must forever remain separate since Eros – seen as self-seeking, self-gratification – must always give way to other-centred love. But *culture has crucified eros*: degrading expressions of *eros* are flaunted on advertising hoardings and cinema screens. Pornography has flooded Eastern Europe since so-called 'liberation'. Yet *eros* at its root meaning is that *yearning, searching for the divine*, that restlessless which Augustine described in the words 'my heart is restless unless it finds its rest in you, O God'.[28] *Eros* is a far wider, far deeper drive than mere self-gratification: it is the basic drive to creativity, joy. It defies reduction and splitting to self- and other-centred loving. Sally Gearhart, describing the power of *eros*, said:

> There is a source, a kind of power, qualitatively different from the one we have been taught to operate with; further, the understanding of the development, the protection of that source and allowing of it to reach full dimensions could mean the redemption of the globe from the devastation of the last thousand years.[29]

The philosopher Whitehead, in his book *Adventures of Ideas*, saw *eros* as the great creative force of history. 'If we omit Psyche and Eros, we have a static world', he wrote.[30] *Eros* is fundamental because it rests in the *eros* of God, the divine yearning for relation out of which the world is created. *Eros* is the inside of everything. 'The divine is always become flesh', wrote Catherine Keller, 'What else does Eros desire?'[31]

But if we trust Eros, because the goal is always Psyche, understood as form, meaning, purpose, intelligence, we have come full circle. The Eros whom Psyche seeks is the divine Eros, is the power of divine love which holds the world together and lures all creation to claim new possibilities.[32]

If Psyche gives Eros form and is the means of transformation, there are valuable clues here for a theology of Church in a fragmented culture. First, there is a need to recreate and recover *soulscapes*, or landscapes for psyche/soul: neither a retreat to dualisms, nor to individualist psychologizing, but the creation of cultural space, visibility, a wholeness which respects human beings in all their needs, hopes and memories, including the cultural memories of specific communities. To give an example: Ireland in 1995 was remembering the Great Hunger, the famine of 150 years ago. When asked to speak on 'The silence of God in the face of the famine' at a conference in Dublin, I discovered that the strongest theme which emerged was the cultural silence surrounding the famine, a silence in which historians and theologians had colluded. The cultural space to remember, to grieve and to seek reparation is the prerequisite for creating soulscape, for visibility for a culture's memory, which has been not so much lost but suppressed.

Secondly, the building blocks for soulscapes, landscapes for the soul, are the drive to relate, the drive to connect, the passion for relation and the mythic imagination. As Hillman writes:

> The opus of the soul needs intimate connection, not only to individuate, but also to live. For this we need relationships of the profoundest kind through which we can realize ourselves, where self-revelation is possible, where interest in and love of soul are paramount, and where eros may move freely, whether it be in analysis, in marriage and family, or between lovers and friends.[33]

Chapter 1 described Etty Hillesum's attempts to create soulscapes through the connecting of interiority with external landscapes. Despite the horror and grief of what was happening as her world broke up, *Psyche never lost touch with Eros*. This points to a third building block for a theology of Church. It is a complete rethinking of the idea of sacrifice. Sacrifice has a bad press in its glorification of violence and suffering in the name of some imagined good, or in privatized 'soul-talk'. But it could be re-imagined rather as Rodolfo Cardenal suggested, in his call for a *culture of austerity* urgently needed in order to bring justice for 'the crucified peoples'.[34] Sacrifice could mean really choosing and living out, whatever the cost, transformed community ideals and values, however counter-cultural. 'Salvation', says the Asian American theologian Rita Brock, who has done so much to locate *eros* not in the individual, but in the community ethic and experience, 'is the healing of life that emerges from our freedom and from the creative imagining of a restored and whole existence.'[35]

Surely this task of *imagining* a restored and whole existence is an agenda for faith community. A debased *eros* separated from culture's soul produced a sick and stultified imagination. The body in pain – and particularly the pain of women and small children – stimulated the imagination in diseased ways, and continues to do so in violent drama and the reporting of crime in the tabloid press. Atrophied imagination sees war as a solution to culture's problems, breeding situations – as in the recent war in Bosnia – where sexual violence was seen as an acceptable accompaniment of militarism. But the *transformed* Christian imagination has a role not just in the passive handing on of tradition, but, stimulated by the mythic imagination, in the reworking and transforming of cultural values. Could we rediscover the power and creativity of a transformed sacramental imagination *to nurture the heart in a broken-hearted world?*

'Till we have faces' functions again as a metaphor of the emergence of sub-cultures within a dominant culture, groups with a story to tell, a language to speak, a history to write – all of which has implications for faith community. Not for nothing did the Jewish writer Emmanuel Levinas, himself an Auschwitz survivor, speak of the significance of the human face in establishing identity, in calling a person out of isolation into relation.

Psyche's last initiatory task was to descend to the Underworld to find a box of Persephone's ointment. Mythic imagination from many cultures tells us that 'the descent into hell' has crucial significance. In Christianity, the Orthodox Church has a great iconic tradition called 'The Harrowing of Hell' – also known as 'The Conquest of Death' – where Jesus descends to release the spirits of the just who have died before him. Orpheus descended to rescue Eurydice, but looked back, and failed. Psyche almost fails, as, against instructions, she opens the box of ointment and falls into a deep sleep. Perhaps something important is going on here, which might offer the key to the recovery of a more biophilic (life-enhancing) culture. Mythically, descending to the underworld is facing death and tragedy, something culture finds very difficult. We *watch* violence daily on the screens, but find it hard to *watch with* dying people, to be present to people living with the daily tragedy of dying with AIDS, to be with the daily suffering of the marginalized gay community. When Psyche returns from the Underworld, she has not conquered death – in the way that Christians see the Resurrection of Jesus as overcoming the power of death – but she has found a way of seeing in the dark and of living with death and destruction. And the ointment signifies both the healing possibilities of living, conscious of death, of not refusing pain.

The nineteenth-century writer George Eliot (Marian Evans) spoke of refusing opium, as a means to experience life intensely.[36] The late – and much mourned – Gillian Rose, a philosopher, suffering from a severe form of cancer, in a brilliant book *Love's Work*,[37] chose as her epigraph the saying from the staretz Silouan, 'Keep your mind in hell, and despair not'. Existence, she wrote, is deprived of its weight, its gravity, when deprived of its agony: 'To grow in love-ability is to accept the boundaries of oneself and others, while remaining vulnerable, woundable, around the bounds.' Ironically, it is when she looks death in the face that Psyche is reunited with Eros – who has also undergone transformation. Reflecting what this might mean culturally, I was once in Paris and, looking in the Louvre Museum, I discovered a photograph of a sculpture of the reunion of Psyche and Eros. To my delight they were looking on each other's faces in full mutuality. They had acquired visibility and full personhood for each other – but they bore the scars of their respective journeys of suffering. They had looked suffering in the face, resisted despair and moved forward.

Facing the same challenges, the complexity of the kinds of journeying needed – 'the road less travelled'[38] – has to be a task for Christian Church.

Notes

1 See *Lumen Gentium*, Constitution on the Church, Chapter VII, in *Vatican Council II: The Conciliar and Post-Conciliar Documents*, ed. Austin Flannery (Dublin: Dominican Publications, 2nd edn 1981); Bishop Bekker, *God's People on the Way* (London: Burns and Oates, 1966). See also its expression in Cardinal Basil Hume, *To Be a Pilgrim* (London: SPCK, 1984).

2 See Catherine de Hueck Doherty, *Poustinia* (London: Collins Fountain Books, 1977).

3 For a contemporary retelling of the story for children, see Arthur Scholey, *Babushka* (Tring: Lion Publishing, 1982).

4 Sigrid Undset, *Kristin Lavransdatter*, tr. Charles Archer (Alfred Knopf, 1923, 1925, 1927; London: Abacus, 1995), p. 257. Of course, the question as to why it is *Kristin*, and not her *husband* who must atone, is not addressed.

5 This was the inspiration I took as the framing myth for *The Wisdom of Fools?* (London: SPCK, 1993).

6 This will be explored in Part Three.

7 James Hillman, *The Myth of Analysis: Three Essays in Archetypal Psychology* (Evanston: Northwestern University Press, 1972), p. 167.

8 I owe this example to my colleague, Dr Andrew Bradstock, whose reflections will appear in his forthcoming book *Nicaragua After the Revolution*.

9 Bradstock, ibid.

10 See M. Grey and R. Zipfel, *From Barriers to Community: The Church in a Divided Society* (London: Collins, 1991).

11 Daphne Hampson, 'Exodus or not?' in *Women Churches: Networking and Reflection in the European Context: Yearbook of the European Society of Women in Theological Research*, vol. III, ed. Angela Berlis, Julie Hopkins, Hedwig Meyer-Wilmes, Caroline Vander Stichele (Kampen: Kok Pharos/Mainz: Matthias Grünewald, 1995), p. 73.

12 Hampson, ibid.

13 Rosemary Radford Ruether, *Women-Church: Theology and Practice* (San Francisco: Harper and Row, 1985), p. 72.

14 Francis Moloney, *A Body Broken for a Broken People* (Melbourne: Collins Dove, 1990).

15 This story was told personally to me by Eva Vörös.

16 Carol Ochs, 'Miriam's Way', *Crosscurrents* 45.4 (Winter 1995–96), pp. 493–509.

17 C. S. Lewis, *Till We Have Faces: A Myth Retold* (London: Collins, Fount Paperback, 1978).

18 Helena Kennedy, *Eve Was Framed!* (London: Chatto and Windus, 1992).

19 In no way am I denying the reality of original sin, trying to assert original innocence or to deny that women and men collude in responsibility for ever-new expression of human sinfulness: I question the enormous burden put on the Adamic myth to guide our understanding of sin, as well as the unequal responsibility which tradition loads onto women. See Angela West, *Deadly Innocence* (London: Mowbray, 1995).

20 Martha Nussbaum, *The Fragility of Goodness* (Oxford: Oxford University Press, 1986).

21 Julia Kristeva, 'Women's time' in *The Kristeva Reader*, tr. Alice Jardine and Harry Blake (Oxford: Blackwell, 1986), pp. 187–213.

22 See Caitlin Matthews, *Sophia, Goddess of Wisdom* (Grafton: HarperCollins, 1991).

23 As Lewis says (*Till We Have Faces*, p. 281): 'Then I looked at Ungit herself. She had not, like most sacred stones, fallen from the sky. The story was that, at the very beginning, she had pushed her way up out of the earth, a foretaste of, or an ambassador from, whatever things may live and work down there ... I have said that she had no face; but that meant that she had a thousand faces. For she was very uneven, lumpy and furrowed, so that, as when we gaze into a fire, you could always see some face or other ... A face as you might see in a loaf, swollen, brooding, infinitely female. "Arnom", said I, whispering, "Who is Ungit?" "I think, Queen," said he, " ... she signifies the earth, which is womb and mother of all living things."'

24 I refer specifically to Europe (though there are parallels in many 'First World' northern hemisphere cultures), because the myth is an ancient European myth. Over-application can dilute the message.

25 James Hillman, *Re-Visioning Psychology* (New York and San Francisco: Harper and Row, 1975); *The Myth of Analysis*, p. 190.

26 It would be a gross over-simplification to pretend that Europe was solely responsible for the whole sex-tourism/pornography/child prostitution rackets. Responsibility is complex. What I ask is that we make the connections between these practices, our flawed understandings of love and the neo-colonial situations in which distortions of *eros* cause extreme suffering.

27 Catherine Keller, *From a Broken Web* (Boston: Beacon, 1986), pp. 156–7.

28 Augustine, *Confessions* 10.27 (London: Collins Fontana, 1957).

29 Sally Gearhart, 'Energy resourcement' in *Women and Values: Readings in Recent Feminist Philosophy*, ed. Marilyn Pearson (Belmont, CA: Wadroth, 1986), pp. 220–30.

30 A. N. Whitehead, *Adventures of Ideas* (London: Macmillan, The Free Press, 1967).

31 Keller, *From a Broken Web*, p. 250.

32 I explored this theme as a theme for the education of girls, in M. Grey, 'Sapiential yearning: the challenge of feminist theology for religious education' in *Christian Theology and Religious Education: Connections and Contradictions*, ed. Jeff Astley and Leslie Francis (London: SPCK, 1996), pp. 78–94.

33 Hillman, *The Myth of Analysis*, p. 192.

34 Rodolfo Cardenal SJ, 'The crucified peoples', Papers of the Inaugural Summer School, *Reclaiming Vision: Education, Liberation and Justice* (Centre for Contemporary Theology, LSU College, Southampton, July 1994).

35 Rita Nakashima Brock, 'The feminist redemption of Christ' in *Christian Feminism: Visions of a New Humanity*, ed. Judith L. Weidman (San Francisco: Harper and Row, 1984), pp. 55–74.

36 George Eliot, 'Letter to Barbara Bodichon'; cited in Brian Spittles, *George Eliot* (London:

Macmillan, 1993), p. 81: 'The highest "calling and election" is to do without opium and live throughout all our pain with conscious, clear-eyed, endurance.'

37 Gillian Rose, *Love's Work* (London: Chatto & Windus, 1995), p. 98.

38 This is the title of the best-selling book by the psycho-therapist M. Scott Peck, *The Road Less Travelled* (London: Rider, 1983).

5

DWELLING: BECOMING AN ECOLOGICAL CHURCH

We dare not deny our role as Churches in the crisis which now overwhelms us. We have not spoken the prophetic word ourselves. Indeed, we did not even hear it when it was spoken by others of late, including a number of scientists. Much less did we hear the cries of indigenous peoples who have told us for centuries that modernity would foul its own nest and even devour its own children. We need to mourn and repent ... We plead for forgiveness and pray for a profound change of heart ... (*Letter to the Churches*[1])

The Church is still preoccupied with individual salvation that ignores earth community; it has become indifferent to widespread use of disruptive technologies that treat nature mechanistically; and it remains acculturated to market economies that promise 'progress' even as they disregard earth-keeping.

(Dieter Hessel[2])

The poignant statement from ecumenical Church leaders on the occasion of the Rio de Janeiro Earth Summit in 1992 (*Letter to the Churches*, above) was an immensely hopeful sign of a growing awareness that becoming Church means taking responsibility for the ecological context in which we dwell. In other words, *dwelling* is an essential part of building community. The soil community, the earth community and the community of all non-human life have for too long been left out of human consciousness, our ethical agendas and our ecclesial living. Whether a theology of Church was approached via the traditional 'marks' of one, holy, catholic, apostolic, or through the dimensions of service, proclamation, worship and community, or through one or other of the Dulles models (see Chapter 2), an ecological consciousness has been tragically lacking. Whatever *journeying* means – as was explored imaginatively in the previous chapter – it certainly does not mean journeying away from the responsibilities of our local bio-region.

Attempts to face this situation usually begin by taking the form of a detailed analysis of the environmental crisis, with statistics on the dying species, overpopulation, polluted air and water and radiation levels, and the lament that the non-renewable resources are running out. I take it as a starting-point that readers of this book are already aware of most of these factors and are already deeply concerned about the planet. What I want to tackle is the sense of inertia and near despair which prevents effective action. Simply knowing the extent of the crisis has not enabled effective action and response. I also want to overcome the resistance that these concerns are not strictly to do with salvation, the care of souls and forgiveness of sins, which is how the Church traditionally interprets its mission. In fact, as Dieter Hessel argues (see above), preoccupation with individual salvation has functioned as a block to a wider sense of responsibilities. This is not for one minute to deny the fact that certain individuals have spoken out prophetically, among whom Pope John Paul II himself is perhaps the most notable,[3] and even Bishops' Conferences have written eloquent statements;[4] but rather I am wrestling with the fact that environmental concerns are still regarded as peripheral to the essence of Church.

Yet becoming community, in any realistic sense, must begin with *where we dwell*. And we dwell on planet earth, in city, village, desert, mountain, forest and lake-side. We dwell in a bio-region with its particular giftedness and its vulnerability to human need and greed. We do not just depend on the earth, *we are the earth*, breathing in her air, drinking her streams and lakes, harvesting her fruit, treading her soil lightly or heavily, depending on what demands we make on our bio-region. As Susan Griffin put it:

> We know ourselves to be made from this earth. We know this earth is made from our bodies. For we see ourselves. And we are nature. We are nature seeing nature. We are nature with a concept of nature. Nature weeping. Nature speaking of nature to nature.[5]

But our heritage of philosophical dualisms has so dulled our sensibilities that we are reluctant to admit our dependence and our vulnerability to nature's graciousness. Indeed, the current fascination with the manufacture of artificial foods, and the ability of the computer to assume numerous functions, have further exacerbated the illusion that the greater the cultural advance, the further *homo sapiens* moves from being nature-dependent. Secondly, that nature is seen as the abode of pagan deities, of animistic sprites, goddesses, the place for the idolatry of trees, Druidic rites, and all that is associated with devil worship, can function – for Christians – as another barrier to a more healthy attitude. 'Nature is to culture as woman is to man' goes the familiar saying,[6] and it is undeniable that nature has been associated with female sexuality by certain strands of Christian tradition which have been equally damaging to both. A third

63

difficulty has been the *anthropocentrism* and indeed *anthroposolism* (coupled with *androcentrism*), which have dominated the Christian tradition,[7] keeping 'man' at the top of the ladder of the great hierarchy of being. As proof of this, it is commonplace to cite the Genesis story of creation where Adam is given the responsibility of naming the creatures (Genesis 2:20). But once the connections are made with the way the Christian Gospel followed in the wake of, for example, the conquistadors of Latin America, then it is clear that – in the crucial historical period when capitalism developed – Christianity became the text underpinning dominance over both nature and indigenous peoples. Thus Frederick Turner described the way Christopher Columbus 'named' the territories he won for Spain in the so-called 'New World':

> To each bit of land he brought the mental map of Europe with which he had sailed. Anciently ... place names arose like rocks and trees out of the contours and colours of the lands themselves ... As a group took up residence in an area, that area would be dotted with names commemorating events that took place in it ... Now came these newest arrivals, but the first names by which they designated the islands were in no way appropriate to the islands themselves. Instead, the Admiral scattered the nomenclature of Christianity over these lands, firing his familiar names like cannonballs against the unresisting New World ... One group was called Los Santos because the Christ-Bearer sailed past them on All Saints' Day. *Armoured Adam in this naked garden, he established dominion by naming.*[8] [My italics]

Small wonder that Mary Daly has made the *power of new naming* central to the self-becoming of women.[9] But animals cannot speak – at least in human language – nature has no voice, and trees make no protest as they are chopped down. Even well-meaning attempts of conscientious Christians to alter the thinking pattern from domination to *stewardship* have not understood the radicality of the change which is needed. Although 'stewardship' rightly stresses care and responsibility for creation, it fails to respect all life-forms for their own sake. Treatment is meted out to animals, plants and trees according to their usefulness to human beings. Usefulness to humanity is presumed to be the point of their existence. We speak of 'beasts of burden' as a genus of animals – and more truly than we realize, it is we ourselves who are the burden! When human beings are described in terms of animals, it is usually a negative description. We eat like wolves or pigs, have 'bird brains', are chicken-hearted, and women are frequently insulted by being called 'cow' or 'bitch'.[10] Although – in the best traditions of post-Enlightenment liberalism – *humane* treatment of animals is advocated (and it is difficult to imagine how fox-hunting can ever be called humane), yet they and other creatures can, it is argued, 'never be members of the moral community'.[11]

So even where Churches call for eco-justice in their best traditions of social justice, it is difficult, as the process theologian John Cobb writes, to break free of their dualistic, modernist heritage:

> My point is that neither 'eco-justice' nor 'sustainable society' necessarily challenges the anthropocentrism and dualism of modern Christianity. Their acceptance was merely the acknowledgement that the condition of the natural world is important for human well-being.[12]

For a theology of Church to explore what it means to dwell on this earth in full appreciation of the value and interdependency of all life-forms, the way forward must be on many fronts. I will discuss three of these. The first is the highlighting of positive strands of Jewish and Christian traditions; the second is to re-interpret the Church's mission ecologically; and the third is to explore the specific ecological revelation of God given when theology is grounded and rooted in the specificity of the bio-region. If our Christian ecclesial life sprang from a conviction that we, along with all members of the earth community, truly *dwell* on this earth, body and spirit, with our histories, memories, hopes and dreams, could there be a transformed theology of *ecclesia*?

To be ecclesia is to be ecological community ... [13]

To recover the *sacramental* dimension of Church is to link with the model which Dulles proposed, but to earth as concretely as possible what is meant by sacrament.[14] It is to be open not only to the richness of the Eastern Orthodox Christian tradition, which has, more than all of our traditions, witnessed to the holiness of God in creation[15] as expressed throughout the range of created life forms. But at the same time it is to mourn that so much of the sacramental *expressions* of the western Church have stifled both our awareness and sense of responsibility to the earth community. The heavens may be telling of the glory of God, as Psalm 19 proclaims, but the actual experience of created realities in contemporary liturgy is minimal. *It is as if we left our bodies at the church door.* The words of sacramental liturgies – bread, wine, oil, salt, water, soil, trees, flowers, fruits of the earth – are evocative of nature. But that is all they are – evocative. Sadly they are rich in promise but empty of ecological connections. We do not make the connections between bread and how it is produced, *who produces it,* who is blessed in the eating of it, and who starves through the lack of it. 'Water gives life', as our sacramental baptismal catechesis teaches, yet huge areas of the world sink into desert, thousands of people in villages in India and in Africa will never know what it means to have running water in their own houses. Through my work in Wells for India I have seen how 'water gives life' means exactly that.[16] As a village gains access to water, the desert turns green and a transformed quality of life is possible. Children have energy to go to school. The women do not have to cross the desert in search of a well which has not dried up and are able to begin spinning, weaving, or planting trees. There is renewed hope that village life is sustainable and that there needs to be no flight to the desperation of pavement life in the cities.

Yet the urgency of *making the ecological connections* within our sacramental life is not rooted in a passing trend; nor does it derive authenticity from the crisis, serious though this certainly is. The ground for enriching sacramental experience is deeply theological. If the Church has credibility in claiming to be sacrament it is because she is the active following of Christ. And to encounter the earthly Jesus was to encounter God.[17] The encounter with the earthly Jesus was an embodied encounter with an itinerant Palestinian Jew from a poor Galilean fishing community, who knew in every fibre of his being the interdependency of all life forms. 'Even the wind and the sea obey him' was the cry (Mark 4:41) – a man who appreciated the beauty of the lilies of the field, the vulnerability of the life of the sparrow, the culture of the vineyard, who knew what it was to toil all night on the lake and catch nothing, who was familiar with the process of breadmaking (Luke 13:20), and the seasons of sowing and reaping. If the metaphor suggested by Sallie McFague and Grace Jantzen is taken seriously, that the world can be experienced as the *Body of God*,[18] then to make interconnections with all the life forms of the bio-region, with food and how it is produced, with the conditions of work in producing it, and with the way that the culture attends to bodily needs, is to meet the concern and compassion of God the Creator.

Our sacramental encounter today is no longer with the earthly Jesus: but discipleship within Christ/Christa community is still *ecological discipleship*. The ecological *ecclesia* is the place where we encounter creation as graced and as blessing, come together to celebrate this, and to respond both to the specific ecological concerns of the bio-region and to responsibilities to wider communities. Postmodernist reading strategies can make us so aware of the *distance* between ourselves and the world of the biblical text that we fail to make the obvious connections. It was remarkable, when journeying through Rajasthan villages, to see how the gynaecological problems of poor women received no attention – they simply did not enter public discourse. This is a culture where taboos exist concerning women speaking with men in public. These women must remain veiled and silent. Yet the earthly Jesus, also in a culture which forbade his talking with women, did not shrink from the encounter with the haemorrhaging woman, an encounter through which she was healed. It can be no accident that so many communities of poor women today are making the connections between the poverty and marginalization from which they now suffer, and the poor communities of New Testament times.[19]

Nor is sacramental encounter about *sanctifying* nature. It is about encountering the holiness already there. The transcendent mystery of God can be glimpsed – but not grasped – by celebrating the material beauty at our fingertips:

> Do you love this world?
>> Do you cherish your humble and silky life?
>>> Do you adore the green grass, with its terror beneath?
>
> Do you also hurry, half-dressed and barefoot, into the garden,
>> and softly,
>>> and exclaiming of their dearness,
>>>> fill your arms with the white and pink flowers,
>
> with their honeyed heaviness, their lush tremblings,
>> their eagerness
>>> to be wild and perfect for a moment, before they are
>>>> nothing, forever?[20]

It is not that we are to worship flowers or trees instead of God. But to feel, to wonder, to give thanks, to be caught in adoration of the sheer grace of nature is to begin to make a response to a God whose own *eros* is expressed by pouring out unceasing love throughout creation, a God for whom *matter matters*. So the challenge in sacramental liturgies is to overcome fear of bodily expression (through liturgical dance, for example), fear of bodily feeling and emotion ('nor can foot feel, being shod', cried Gerard Manley Hopkins),[21] and to understand the encounter with Christ as communion and connectedness with all life-forms as graced. Joy and delight in these connections give a way back to a deep knowing and reverence of the meaning of holiness in creation. At the same time, this sacramental hallowing *could be the way to recovering soul*: for it becomes part of gathering the fragments, the knitting together of body and soul. Sacramental hallowing has to be understood again as *leitourgia*, liturgy, the work of the people. It is a task to which not the theologians, but poets, artists and musicians have been more faithful – not forgetting the mystics, despite the fact that the mystical strand of religious traditions has been ambiguous as regards hallowing creation and bodiliness. John Haught pointed out that

> mysticism disassociated from a vigorous sacramentalism promotes the gnostic

doctrine of 'cosmic homelessness' ... Mysticism can be so greedy for the other world at times that it splits off from its matrix in sacramentalism.[22]

Believing in 'cosmic homelessness' – that our true home lies beyond the universe – has had a devastating effect on Christian theology's response to the ecological crisis. It is the pervasive conviction that even if the earth plunges into ecological ruin, ultimately it is of no account, because our real home is in heaven, beyond the earth. What is more, spoilt patriarchal children that we are, we fondly expect that 'Daddy will give us a new one'.[23] The earth, like paper handkerchiefs, is disposable. But the mystical dimension of religion need not locate itself in otherness and the beyond. Rather, it points to God revealed in the strangeness and majesty in creation as well as the homely earthiness. The ecological mystic today is not so much the beholder of bright lights and voices – which is in any case a caricature of mysticism: mysticism is the vision of the wholeness and interconnectedness of creation, as caught up in the presence and sustaining love of God. But it is a vision to which the whole *ecclesia* is called. The late Trappist monk Thomas Merton experienced this *epiphany of connectedness*, in a trip to the town of Louisville:

> In Louisville ... in the center of the shopping district, I was suddenly over-whelmed with the realization that I loved all those people, that they were mine and I theirs, that we could not be alien to one another even though we were total strangers. It was like waking from a dream of separateness, of spurious isolation in a special world, the world of renunciation and supposed holiness ... I have the immense joy of being ... a member of a race in which God Himself became incarnate ... There is no way of telling people that they are walking round shining like the sun.[24]

This experience can be multiplied from contexts as diverse as ecofeminist creation spiritualities and Buddhist mysticism. But mysticism as *community response* to creation is a profound – if hidden – strand of *Christian* theology. The mystic can be silent, contemplative – but can also be filled with exhilaration and overcome by the sheer humour of life. I do not imagine that the twelfth-century Hildegarde of Bingen, when she dressed her sisters in beautiful gowns and crowns, in celebration of virginity, was unaware of the funny side of this. And the fact that her reaction to her visions, which she received from the age of five years, was to make her hymns and the singing of the Office the central point of community life, points to the fact that mysticism, community and the liturgical celebration of beauty are all linked.[25]

This leads to the next strand. To experience the ecological Christ as communion with all life forms is to encounter tragic situations where humanity, animals and soil community alike struggle for survival. The temptation is to lose faith and hope. But the God of the covenant reminds us of the fidelity promised to creation throughout the Hebrew Scripture. Even before the covenant with Abraham, the covenant with Noah after the Flood promised that 'While the earth remains, seedtime and harvest, cold and heat, summer and winter, day and night, shall not cease' (Genesis 8:22). The rainbow was the sign of this everlasting covenant. When the *fact* of the radical faithfulness of God to creation is linked with the *metaphor* of the world as the Body of God, it becomes clear that the death of the species, the ravaging of the earth's surface, are all wounds in the Body of God. God's pain is the earth's pain. But all the ravaging does not take away from the solid bedrock of fidelity which is the very being of God. It is human beings who constantly renege on and rupture the covenantal relationship. It seems as if the birds and the beasts are more faithful than we are: as Job in all his pain cried out:

> But ask the beasts, and they will teach you;
> the birds of the air, and they will tell you;
> or the plants of the earth and they will teach you;
> and the fish of the sea will declare to you.
> Who among all these does not know
> that the hand of the Lord has done this? (Job 12:7–9)

Jesus, from deep within the Jewish covenantal relationship, proclaimed a new covenant. What could he have meant by 'new covenant', understood ecologically? When Jesus speaks of fidelity it is in the context of radical fidelity to the demands of the Kingdom of God. It is just not acceptable to place the ties of family or property first. The great vision of the Kingdom of God means the reordering of relations between women, men, children and nature. The passion for justice which drove Jesus and continues to drive Christ community is a passion for justice for all forms of life. The fact of his death on the Cross showed that Jesus gave the last breath of life and energy believing in this great dream of life restored and renewed: and the hallmark of discipleship is that we follow him and are present where the suffering of the cosmos is at its most acute. But this is not because we choose to suffer or wallow in a glorification of pain. Larry Rasmussen, in a moving and sensitive essay, showed that the places of suffering creation were also the places where the power of Cross and Resurrection would be manifest:

> until our pain is intensified at the sight of creation's pain, as God's is, there is no redemption . . . until we enter the places of suffering and experience them with those entangled there, as God does, our actions will not be co-redemptive.[26]

This is exactly the point for *ecological ecclesia*, showing where the focus of activity should be, and where the power of God's activity will be manifest. Rasmussen argues that power that does not go to the places where community and creation are most obviously ruptured and ruined is no power for healing at all:

> The only power that can truly heal and keep the creation is power drawn instinctively to the *flawed places of existence*, there to call forth from the desperate and the needy themselves extraordinary yet common powers that they did not even know they had.[27] [My italics]

This new covenant of fidelity, rooted in the flourishing of the Kingdom of God, has a radical inclusivity which our imaginations up till now have not been able to fathom. But it is more a failure of our imaginations and hierarchies of concerns than it is of prophetic justice. The new covenant in Jesus can be seen as calling us back to the deeper meaning of the Jewish covenant. It deepens our understanding of the core of prophetic justice. For the message of the prophets certainly had a strong ecological dimension. Time and again Isaiah linked the restoration of Israel's fortunes with the restoration of the land, conversion and repentance with the healing of the ravaged land, justice with the proper treatment of the land, ecological damage with a failure to 'know the Lord'.[28]

Even if the Hebrew prophets did not make the links we make now between the suffering of poor women and ecological devastation, centuries of Christian thought also failed to make these links. But now the mission of *ecological ecclesia* cannot ignore the making of these connections and the actions which they urge. For the radical inclusivity of the covenant relationship to which we are called is an ethical challenge to become sensitive to all forms of pain, to all struggles to maintain and nurture life, and *to give a priority to the most vulnerable*.

Mission and ecology

Rasmussen's sensitive call to direct our efforts to the 'flawed places of existence' is a challenge to rethink the priorities of what it means to be Church. These highlight the need for the Church's mission to be put in an ecological context, which was exactly the vision which the *Letter to the Churches* from Rio tried to rekindle.

The Church has always understood mission as the command to preach the Gospel to the ends of the earth.[29] But at the heart of this understanding is fidelity to Jesus' proclamation that *the poor would have the good news preached to them* (Luke 4:18–30). It is the poor, understood as poor women, indigenous peoples, vulnerable and abused children, rejected elderly people, people with AIDS, refugees and homeless people, the long-term unemployed, the mentally handicapped, political prisoners, those marginalized for race, sexual preference and religion – these all fall within the biblical category of the 'poor' and rightly call for compassion and justice. They dwell at the 'flawed places of existence' – in shop doorways, under bridges, on the roads fleeing persecution, in neglected housing developments, in poorly resourced psychiatric hospitals, or cleaning office blocks late at night. There is another category of the 'spiritually poor' which includes the economically rich, who are deprived of spiritual resources, who suffer from broken relationships, and the pressures of the professional rat race. Christian social thinkers are well aware of the danger of the focus shifting to the needs of the 'spiritually poor' to the detriment of those who are in desperate need of political and economic justice.

But if mission is about 'being sent', then the 'flawed places of existence' must be where the heart of Christian discipleship must gather and focus its attention: it is here that awareness awaits us that the suffering of nature and poor people are intimately interwoven. Where the Amazonian forest is destroyed, the Yanomani Indians are homeless and their very survival is threatened. The Chernobyl disaster killed off a whole bio-region, and blighted a generation of children with leukaemia. In certain drought-stricken villages of Rajasthan which we have surveyed, over half the children die before the age of five through water-related diseases. But the point is not to direct concern to nature in order to save only the human community. The shift in thinking to make is that the well-being and survival of both belong together. We do not reclaim the desert or fight pollution only for our enjoyment, or to make only human life sustainable. For too long the blindness which the image of the Great Chain of Being caused[30] – a pyramid where 'man' is perched imperialistically at the top, and so-called 'lower' forms of life in descending rungs to the bottom – has prevented us from valuing other forms for their own sake, and for the sake of the Creator. We flourish and die together. Third World women theologians have been pointing this out for years, especially as part of the World Council of Church's Process, Justice, Peace and Integrity of Creation,[31] but now, at last, liberation theologians have woken up to the fact that the struggle for justice must include the struggle to halt environmental degradation – though this is frequently still at the level of saving the earth in order to save the people.[32]

What gives enormous hope is that what the churches are good at is the practice of pastoral care. Not only is there a constant tradition that *cura animarum* has always included healing in its widest interpretation, but Christian missionary thinking has shown its ability to adapt and reinterpret its focus.

There has been a massive volte-face and repentance – alas, not yet total – from a colonial and imperialistic, mission theology, where Eurocentric and paternalistic theologies and patterns of pastoral care were exported to conquered territories. The stress now is far more on supporting indigenous community struggles, understanding a community's self-defined need and discovering appropriate forms of solidarity. The learning which results is often mutually beneficial. There is often a built-in ecological understanding and respect for the rhythms of the earth among poorer communities of the South, from which Northerners need to learn.

Secondly, the Church as *teacher* can extend its understanding of truth to *ecological truth*. Instead of proclaiming the limitless possibilities of being human, the Church can show how by listening and learning from the patterns of nature, humanity has to rediscover its own limits and finitude. The Church already has a framework for this in the liturgical year which follows the seasons. (Although there is again a need to lose the fear of association with paganism, by a too-close association with the rhythms of nature: perhaps the creativity of creation spiritualities can lead a way forward.) Thirdly, the Church as *Mother* is often interpreted in a way which fosters passive dependency, or in a way which subtly disempowers our earthly mothers.[33] But for the Church to be Mother is to deepen the notion of caring. As Mary Evelyn Jegen points out: 'The characteristic quality of our mother the church is caring. It may surprise us to discover that the word "care" includes the notion of anxiety for another, an attention marked by strong emotion.'[34] She links the role of caring with the notion of contemplation. To relate to the world through a *caring contemplation* provides a way forward from simply regarding it as a backdrop for human activity. A caring contemplation is far more than gazing at the sunrise. It is an active contemplation, fuelled by a tenderness towards other life forms. But the Church as Mother is also at the heart of what Beatrice Bruteau calls the 'theotokos project'.[35] The cosmos itself is caught up in the great movement of bringing God to birth, the cosmos itself is Godbearer:

> The metaphor of the female Godbearer gives us another theme . . . and that is the sense of gestation, of gradual formation and emergence. The divine is hidden in the body of the material world, where it grows secretly, in terms of its own internal programs of formation, until it can be birthed into full visibility.[36]

The Church is Mother, in the caring attention given to this great birthing project of God. In fact, she is more accurately *midwife* to the process, since God's is always the initiative in grace. What a different context is given to evangelization and mission, if the priority is put, not on commanding what ought to be done, in insisting on control from the top, but on paying attention to the interdependence of all life-communities, on teaching their goodness, on working for their survival on healing the wounds of the planet, and on facilitating the bringing to birth of new harmonies between people and nature: as the Book of Revelation put it, 'And the leaves of the tree were for the healing of the nations' (Revelation 22:2).

Dwelling and divine epiphany

This chapter has been stressing *dwelling* as a dimension of being Church. But in addition to the Church's renewed self-understanding in terms of ecological mission, and as well as the reclaiming of ecological dimensions of sacrament, covenant and the mystical tradition, there is another aspect of dwelling, which is the revelation or epiphany of God given when we explore where we dwell as the *locus of divine gift and presence.*[37] Too often, relating to nature and the environment is understood simplistically, as a means to revitalize flagging human energies by, for example, a 'romp on the beach or watching the sunrise'.[38] But if it is taken seriously that the universe is God's artwork, that the whole world is the body of God, or *the arena of the embodying of God*, as I have been arguing, then revelation is far more than a set of propositions to be adhered to, but a daily drama of the unfolding of God's embodiment.[39] And we are actors in this drama, a drama which has both cosmic and tragic dimensions.

Given that every diverse context carries a rich potential for *journeying into God*, the focus of Christian *ecclesia*, I explore here the diversity of garden, desert and city as places where we experience the embodying of God. Who, then, is the God revealed to us in the garden? Indisputably, a prominent strand in both Jewish and Christian traditions that creation took specific form and shape in the Garden of Eden tells us that here God walked with Adam and Eve: the presence of the divine to the human in the richness of creation is striking. Here they received the charge to care for creation, and understood creation as blessed in all life forms. The blessedness and sheer graced quality of creation was witnessed to partly by keeping the Sabbath: thus part of the fragmentation from which society suffers today (see Part One), is that Sabbath holiness is usually celebrated – as I have observed – not by liturgies of praise, but by shopping, cleaning the car, or receiving the word of the *Sunday Times*, instead of the Gospel of Good News!

But here I explore the meaning of the God given to us in the garden in a much more practical sense. Whether the garden means a window box on a

73

balcony, an allotment, a real market garden, a small back garden, or the municipal parks, there is a richness of embodied divine presence offered here. First, the work needed for plants to grow – pruning, mulching, weeding, sowing, watering – is actually the work of co-creating with all the energies of nature. Nothing grows without the mixture of labour and grace, a metaphor for the 'theotokos project' of birthing creation. With our hands deep in the earth we human beings learn dependence – body, soul and spirit – on nature's gifts for our very survival. And we learn this in the specificity of the bio-region. Oranges and lemons in the Mediterranean, mangoes in Trinidad, strawberries in Britain and bananas in Africa are the tangible gifts of nature's specificity.[40] From the God of the garden comes awareness of sheer overwhelming diversity of creation in the rhythm of the seasons' sequence. The mutual nature of gift and response as a basic life rhythm enters into the fibre of our being as the energy poured out in digging and watering is balanced by the quiet delight in plants growing and the satisfaction of harvesting.[41] The lesson of our very fragility and the limits of human existence can be accepted better as humanity learns its place within the life-cycles of many species. One of the simplest and most fundamental Gospel messages has been: 'Unless a grain of wheat falls into the earth and dies, it remains alone; but if it dies, it bears much fruit' (John 12:24). Whatever the truth about the immortality of the human soul and the promise of eternal life, the lesson we have first to learn is that humanity shares with all living organisms an existence both temporal and material, and the cycles of birth and death. The God of the garden teaches us to let go of earthly existence graciously, yet at the same time to delight in its richness, diversity and sheer givenness. To learn that perpetual existence is not an inalienable right of human beings – 'Is anything solved by my surviving forever?' asked Wittgenstein – can both teach us to be aware of the tragic dimension of cosmic existence, and stimulate us to listen also to the *crying of the earth*, the great need for justice of the earth communities of soil, air and water.[42] While not underestimating the moral responsibility which human beings have with regard to other species in respect of vulnerability, fragility and dependence, we stand organically related to all living things.

But most people do not live in gardens or the countryside but in cities. Christianity originated as an urban religion, in contrast with the *pagani*, who were country-dwellers. The need to become *ecological ecclesia* in the city is no less urgent today. The problems of Calcutta, Bombay, Cairo, São Paulo and Mexico, overwhelming as they are, are directly related to the situation in the villages. To eke out a desperate existence on the pavements of Calcutta has become the only option for survival for many poor Indians because life in the village was no longer sustainable.[43] Yet, ironically, cities have expressed most lyrically both human dreaming and the concrete attempts to create cosmopolitan communities of justice. The 'holy cities', the 'cities of dreams', of 'dreaming spires', cities where emperors and dynasties have given concrete expression to ambition and dreams of glory, achieved usually by the blood, sweat and tears of slaves and poor people – these abound. Cities as seedbeds of crime, as places of violence and fear, of the corruption of children and young people – these also abound.

Nor is the contrast between village and city so absolute: in the city centre of Ajmer, in Rajasthan (north-west India), in the height of rush hour I watched the traffic come to a halt as, in the middle of a big roundabout, it was time to feed the cows – who wander freely through the city in any case. Two rhythms were in sharp contrast: the lazy movements of the cows, peacefully munching their way through the hay given to them, and the furious bustle of the taxis, rickshaws, bicycles, buses, who were all forced to halt, were in conflict with each other. It was a striking symbol that the interdependence of all living things is the same for dwellers of city or village alike. It is the huge needs of the concentrated mass of people, traditionally kept pacified by various versions of the bread and circuses invented by the Roman emperors, which block the basic need for an *ecology of the city*, for growing things, open spaces, clean air, unpolluted water, responsibility for ecological waste disposal and recycling, and awareness of interdependence with the earth communities. Because the glittering shopping malls and the National Lottery have become today's versions of bread and circuses, with the added problem that supermarkets are able – in many parts of Western Europe and North America – to offer produce out of season from all parts of the world, consciousness has become dulled as to what grows where – and in what season.

But cities are also powerful expressions of symbols of power, of what human beings consider precious, be it now Stock Exchange, cyber café, video shop or war memorial. In this postmodern world there is a bizarre juxtaposition of what is held sacred: Christian churches can easily become Sikh temples or nightclubs. Yet because cities are places where poverty and human misery are most evident, it is here that the struggle and commitment to justice must be focused.[44] God revealed as *passion for justice-making* is the unique revelation given in the city. In an interesting exchange of letters between Rosemary Radford Ruether, a young theologian just beginning her career, and the Trappist monk Thomas Merton, a year before his death, this was exactly the point of tension.[45] Ruether then regarded monasticism as escapism, since the commitment to social justice is only authentic if it is tackling inner city problems:

For those who want to be at the 'kingdom' frontier of history, it is the steaming ghetto of my big city, not the countryside that is the radical overcoming of this world, the place where one renews creation.[46]

Even Merton's spirited defence of monasticism – that the monk not only changes the world theologically, but literally, because he protects the world from 'the destructiveness of the rampaging city of greed' (p. 35) – is rejected by Ruether. For her, the *shalom* of the Kingdom, lions lying down with lambs, will only be realized through historical redemption, through 'struggling with the powers and principalities where they really are', not by taking off into the hills (p. 41).

The tension in this interchange illustrates the point I am making. For, 28 years later, Rosemary Ruether, involved in the struggles against many interlocking oppressions, is also a pioneer in ecological theology.[47] Yet Thomas Merton, long after his death, has become an inspiration for movements for peace and social justice. For the Church what matters is that ecological concerns are the Church's concern, be the dwelling garden, city or desert. The God who comes with such energy for justice in the city, the Christ who walks with the homeless, sleeping under the bridges, the Spirit building community in department stores and market places, is the God given when we work for just relation, when just relational power[48] is tangibly present, where authentic community is constructed with prisoners, addicts and the homeless. Edwina Gateley, in her work with the prostitutes of Chicago, shows both the strength and fragility of relational power in action. Dorothy Day, who discovered real joy in creation and ecological sensitivity during her brief time on Staten Island, poured all her energies into creating communities in the inner cities and struggling against poverty. Jim Wallis and the Sojourners Community in Washington, protesting against all forms of injustice, are powerful witness that the God who is passion for justice still keeps vision and imagination alive amidst degradation and despair.[49]

And the God of the desert? Can this God be present wherever we dwell? How is God present to those who dwell in actual desert, for whom this desert is experienced as harshness, a place where women must walk in the burning sun in search of water? A desert which has been created by deforestation? Or of blessed solitude, when one is stripped of all but what is essential? 'But what did you go out into the desert to see?' Or is the desert that of the inner city, where community has become an impossible dream? The revelation of God offered through the metaphor of desert-dwelling is that of the basic simplicity and emptiness which enables awareness of the presence of God. In the *caring contemplation* which is what an ecological spirituality offers, getting rid of all that is superfluous and excessive enables us simply to pay attention, to be attentive to all that is true, of value, and thus of God. Wordiness in worship has often prevented appreciation of silence. Yet many young people who climb the mountain to Taizé discover a joy in the prayer of silence. In this, the Dark Night of the Church, could a way through be offered here, a means of discovering authentic *ecclesia* in the cultural desert which modern living often means? *Inheriting Our Mothers' Gardens* – the title of an inspirational collection of essays linking search for mother, ecological concern and the struggle for liberation – has become a privileged symbol in feminist theology, connecting the power of growing things with the creativity of our foremothers and their struggle to survive.[50]

So paying attention to where we dwell, as an ecological spirituality, means being receptive to God's presence, in the concrete situation of garden, city, desert (or forest, mountain, factory or multi-national). I have focused on the former three because they have a long tradition within Christianity and Judaism as the privileged places where God spoke to the children of Israel. And it is to the question of what kind of tradition, and attitude to it, will lead the Church out of the Dark Night that I now turn.

Notes

1 *Letter to the Churches* (Geneva: WCC, 1992), p. 10.

2 Dieter Hessel (ed.), *After Nature's Revolt: Eco-justice and Theology* (Minneapolis: Fortress, 1992), Introduction, p. 13.

3 See for example, *Centesimus Annus* (Vatican City, May 1991), pp. 37–8.

4 For example, Joint Pastoral Letter by the Guatemalan Bishops' Conference (1987) in *Newsletter* (Toronto: InterChurch Committee on Human Rights in Latin America, 1988); Catholic Bishops of the Dominican Republic, *The Protection of Nature in a Condition of Survival* (1987), quoted in *Renewing the Earth* (CAFOD Campaign, 1989–1991). An excellent source for these is Sean McDonagh, *The Greening of the Church* (London: Geoffrey Chapman/Maryknoll: Orbis, 1990).

5 Susan Griffin, *Woman and Nature: The Roaring Inside Her* (New York: Harper and Row, 1978).

6 See Sherry Ortner, 'Is female to male as nature is to culture?' in *Women, Culture and Society*, ed. M. Z. Rosaldo and L. Lamphere (Stanford, CA: Stanford University Press, 1974). Also see discussion of this in Catharina Halkes, *New Creation* (London: SPCK, 1991), ch. 1.

7 To clarify these terms: *anthropocentrism* means a focus on humanity, subordinating the other life forms; *anthroposolism* means a focus on humanity to the exclusion of the other life forms; *androcentrism* means a focus on maleness as the norm for humanity.

8 Frederick Turner, *Beyond Geography: The Western Spirit Against the Wilderness* (New Brunswick, NJ: Rutgers University Press, 1986), p. 131.

9 Originally expressed in Mary Daly, *Beyond God the Father* (Boston: Beacon, 1973), but now

found everywhere in the genre of feminist spiritual quest.

10 The link between insulting epithets of animals and women is well made by Carol Adams, *Neither Man Nor Beast* (New York: Continuum, 1989).

11 This has been powerfully and recently argued by Roger Scruton, *Animal Rights and Wrongs* (London: Demos, 1996). See review in the *Times Higher Education Supplement* (*THES*) (5 July 1996), and my reply (26 July).

12 John Cobb, 'Postmodern Christianity and eco-justice' in Hessel, *After Nature's Revolt*, p. 28.

13 Some of the strands which I develop here have also been discussed by others, but not in an attempt to construct an ecological theology of Church. For example, Rosemary Ruether discusses the covenantal and sacramental traditions in *Gaia and God* (San Francisco: HarperCollins, 1993); Catharina Halkes examines the Sabbath traditions in *New Creation*; John Haught in *The Promise of Nature: Ecology and Cosmic Purpose* (New York: Paulist, 1993) discusses the mystical, sacramental, eschatological and covenantal aspects. Prophetic justice is frequently discussed in the context of eco-justice and the Jubilee traditions.

14 See Ruether, *Gaia and God*, ch. 9, pp. 229–53; and Haught, *The Promise of Nature*, pp. 76–80.

15 See, for example, Paulos Gregorios, *Ecological Spirituality and the Age of the Spirit* (New York: Amity, 1987).

16 See Preface, note 6 (p. viii above).

17 See E. Schillebeeckx, *Christ, the Sacrament of the Encounter with God* (London: Sheed and Ward, 1963).

18 See Sallie McFague, *The Body of God* (London: SCM, 1993); Grace Jantzen, *God's World, God's Body* (London: Darton, Longman and Todd, 1984).

19 John Pobee and Bårbel Wartenberg Potter (eds), *New Eyes for Reading* (Geneva: WCC, 1986).

20 Mary Oliver, 'Peonies' in *New and Selected Poems* (Boston: Beacon, 1992); cited in Douglas Burton-Christie, 'Nature, spirit and imagination in the poetry of Mary Oliver', *Crosscurrents* (Spring 1996), p. 85.

21 See Gerard Manley Hopkins, 'God's Grandeur' in *Poems* (London: Penguin, 1953), p. 27.

22 Haught, *The Promise of Nature*, p. 80.

23 The phrase is Catherine Keller's: see 'The greening of the weather' in *Reweaving the World: The Emergence of Ecofeminism*, ed. Irene Diamond and Gloria Fernan Orenstein (San Francisco: Sierra Club, 1990).

24 Thomas Merton, *Conjectures of a Guilty Bystander* (London: Burns and Oates, 1965, 1995), pp. 156–7.

25 The best source on the life of Hildegarde of Bingen is Barbara Newman, *Sister of Wisdom* (Berkeley: University of California/Scolar Press, 1987).

26 Larry Rasmussen, 'Returning to our senses: the theology of the cross as a theology for eco-justice' in Hessel, *After Nature's Revolt*, p. 49.

27 Ibid., p. 49. In an extended footnote (21) Rasmussen sensitively deals with the problem that to make the cross symbol so central – as is mandatory in Lutheran ethics – seems to join in with legitimizing suffering. But this is certainly not his intention. What kind of power this should be – in order to transform the flawed places – will be the subject of a later chapter.

28 For example, Isaiah 11:6–9; 24:3–13; 25:6–8; 35:1–10; 43:18–21; 65:17–25.

29 See *The Catechism of the Catholic Church* (London: Geoffrey Chapman, 1994).

30 For a discussion of the harm which this image has caused throughout Christian tradition, and for an alternative metaphor, see Paul Santmire, *The Travail of Nature* (Philadelphia: Fortress, 1985).

31 See Elisabeth Gerle, *The Search for a Global Ethic* (Lund Studies in Ethics and Theology 2; series ed. Göran Bexell; Lund: Lund University Press, 1995).

32 For example, Leonardo Boff in *Ecology and Liberation: A New Paradigm*, tr. John Cumming (Maryknoll: Orbis, 1995).

33 There is also a confusion between the role of the Church and the role of Mary as Mother: there do seem to be a profusion of mothers!

34 Mary Evelyn Jegen, 'The Church's role in caring for the earth' in Wesley Granberg Michaelson (ed.), *Tending the Garden: Essays on the Gospel and the Earth* (Grand Rapids: Eerdmans, 1987), p. 100.

35 Beatrice Bruteau, 'The theotokos project' in *Embracing Earth: Catholic Approaches to Ecology*, ed. Albert LaChance and John Carroll (Maryknoll: Orbis, 1994), pp. 53–75.

36 Ibid., p. 57.

37 Although this belongs also to the 'Spirituality' chapter, it is a vital part of 'dwelling', especially in the light of what has been said in connection with the 'theotokos project'.

38 The phrase is Rosemary Ruether's.

39 In *The Wisdom of Fools?* (London: SPCK, 1993), I attempted to explore revelation through the metaphor of connectedness.

40 I am aware that the predominance of multi-national methods of trading now means that everything is available in the supermarkets of the North – but not in the South – in all seasons. This also blurs the distinct gifts of different seasons.

41 I realize I refer here to a privileged situation where, in the North, we can rely on water to irrigate our crops. Nor does the success of our particular efforts usually mean the difference between life and death. Where the very possibility of a crop is under threat, where labour involves unjust conditions, where survival is threatened – then there is a vastly different presence of God.

42 See Alvin Pitcher, *Listen to the Crying of the Earth: Cultivating Creation Communities* (Cleveland: The Pilgrim Press, 1993).

43 See Dominic Lapierre, *City of Joy* (London: Arrow, 1986).

44 This will be the focus of Chapter 7, 'Transforming'.

45 Mary Tardiff OP (ed.), *At Home in the World: The Letters of Thomas Merton and Rosemary Ruether* (Maryknoll: Orbis, 1995), with Introduction by Rosemary Ruether.

46 Ibid., p. 20. See also M. Grey, 'Escape the world or change the world? Towards a feminist theology of contemplation', *Proceedings of the International Thomas Merton Conference* (1996).

47 See Rosemary Ruether, *Gaia and God*.

48 Relational power will be discussed in Chapter 10.

49 For the vision of Jim Wallis, see *The Soul of Politics* (San Diego: Harcourt Brace and Co., 1994).

50 The phrase is Alice Walker's: *In Search of Our Mothers' Gardens* (San Diego: Harcourt Brace Jovanovich, 1983); but it provided inspiration for Letty Russell, Katy Cannon, Kwok Pui Lan *et al.*, *Inheriting Our Mothers' Gardens* (Louisville, KY: Westminster, 1988).

6

TRADITIONING

Feminists are not alone in raising questions that go to the very heart of the Christian tradition. The question of the uniqueness of Jesus Christ as revelation of God faces many other Christian theologians who are attempting to rethink traditional Christian claims in the context of the reunions of the world. The questions of normative Christian liturgical symbols and appropriate leadership at liturgy are being raised in diverse situations of enculturation around the globe. More fundamental are the issues of fidelity and identity. As Christians claiming our baptism we commit ourselves to the God revealed in Jesus Christ in and through the power of the Spirit, to a life of discipleship, to fidelity to the Gospel and the apostolic tradition, to communion with the universal Church. As feminists we also make explicit our basic commitment to the full life and dignity of every woman, man and child and to the flourishing of creation. Feminist Catholics continue to hope that the revelation of God among us may be discovered in the intersection of those commitments.

(Mary Catherine Hilkert[1])

When the Church of England Synod voted for the ordination of women to the priesthood on 11 November 1992, amidst the euphoria of those who had campaigned for so long for this to happen, a storm of protest burst out from many quarters. This was a divisive move for Church unity, went the protest. Furthermore, it was an illegitimate move even for the Church of England itself to vote unilaterally without the support of the full Anglican Communion. It evoked such a confusion of identity, of authority and truth, and a questioning as to the meaning of ordained priesthood that many Anglican priests felt obliged to move to the Roman Catholic Church.[2] (This of course was balanced to some extent by the movement in the other direction.) The pain of those Church of England priests upset by the vote to a large extent eclipsed the pain of the women who had been excluded for so long and who continued to experience discrimination, together with the continuing anguish of the Roman Catholic women around the world for whom no change loomed on the horizon.

Again appeared the age-old accusation – that women were guilty of rocking the boat, of seeking power, of blocking Church unity and most of all, of *disturbing tradition*. As successive papal statements of the last twenty years have made clear, the Roman Catholic Church has never ordained women, never will, and does not feel it in her power to do so.[3] Such is the rigidity and unshakeability of tradition – at least in this understanding of it.

But is this the one way to understand tradition? Is there not an urgent need, already referred to by Mark Kline Taylor as one of the horns of the postmodern trilemma (see Chapter 3), to develop a richer, more positive and creative attitude to tradition? So often tradition appears to be a crushing burden on our shoulders which we have to carry from one age to the next: instead of the living faith of a dead people, it frequently seems to be *the dead faith of a living people*.[4] The breaking of tradition – in the form of a Christian marrying a Jew – threatened the core of the identity of the little Russian Jewish community of Anatevka, in the famous play *Fiddler on the Roof*. In Chaim Potok's novel about the career of the young Jewish painter Asher Lev, it was in defying the Hasidic prohibition against depicting images, and in defying tradition by using a *Christian* symbol (painting his mother on a cross), which caused the crisis in which Asher Lev was thrown out of the community.[5] In both these cases there was an outright defiance of rules which threatened the precarious identity of a community struggling through difficult times. This throws up the idea that rigid adherence to tradition is as much about preserving identity under threat, as it is about theological truth.[6]

Secondly, if we could orient ourselves to tradition less as a burden, and more as positive resource, an orientation towards the future, then new possibilities emerge. As the Russian Orthodox theologian Elisabeth Behr-Sigel wrote,

> Sometimes tradition even seems frozen under a great ice shell but below this frozen and rigid surface flow ever fresh springtime waters. It is up to us, with the help of God's grace, to break the ice that is above all the ice of our hearts become cold . . . From the ancient spring we will drink water that will give us a new force so as to answer the questions of today.[7]

In *The Wisdom of Fools?* I tried to re-image tradition organically as *nurturing and sustaining memory*. Here I develop this, using the metaphor of dipping into the well or spring of fresh water to rediscover tradition positively as a dimension of *relational and ecological ecclesia*. For a relational theology cannot submit to the narcissism of the present moment, unique and intoxicating though this may be. Relational intensity is more than Eliot's 'a lifetime burning in every moment';[8] relational *ecclesia* seeks, as a matter of justice and of truth, to relate to the past, through a positive attitude to tradition. It seeks creatively to *carry the past forward to the future*. Ironically, though postmodernism has cast suspicion on the grand stories and the universal patterns, yet in turning us back to the specific context in which we are faithful to Christian community, traditions, culture, oral history, ritual and symbol have all acquired new significance and respect. Pilgrimages to local shrines have never been more popular (see Chapter 4, 'Journeying'). Geneticists make increasing discoveries of the influence of genes on human identity – a purely chemical way of stressing debt to the past. Archetypal memories, too, play their part – as will be discussed later. *Reality* has itself become a suspect word, linked with power, and with those responsible for the dominant story. Furthermore, reality has become a fantasy, a cocoon, that the narcissistic 'I' creates around 'him'. In this 'one brief shining moment', this disposable pleasure-dome, there is no past. More opulent versions of Disneyland are the only future.

Never has there been a greater need for the recovery of solidarity with the past struggles to create authentic *ecclesia*, communities of justice, of truth and fidelity to the vision of the Kingdom of God. So language, power, memory, so-called cultural amnesia of suffering and oppression, gaps and silences – are all strands to be woven into this attempt to recover what has been called 'the search for a usable past',[9] the recovery of tradition as *nurturing memory* and resource for a different ethics of *ecclesia*.

'If I was you, I wouldn't start from here': getting the starting-point right

Because feminist theology like all liberation theologies focuses on who has been left out, marginalized, silenced, forgotten, the problem arises with regard to tradition *as to what authority is appealed to*, in inserting the silenced voices into mainstream tradition. What should be the relation of, for example, Hagar, who is enormously inspirational for womanist theology, the black-led women churches and for Third World women in general,[10] to the central symbols of Christian faith, the 'central' characters in the story of dying and rising? Does the fact that for Woman-Church,[11] the terrible story of the concubine of Judges 19 takes central place in liturgies condemning and mourning violence against women, automatically give it a privileged place for an *ecclesia* of justice-making?[12] In other words, is the reclaiming and proclaiming process completely arbitrary?

A sure starting-point for Roman Catholic feminists is the widened notion of revelation issuing from the Second Vatican Council. The Constitution on Revelation, *Dei Verbum*, makes it clear that what is handed on (*traditum*), includes everything which contributes to the holiness of life, and the increase of faith of the People of God; and so the Church, in her teaching, life, and worship, perpetuates and hands on to all generations all that she herself is, all that she believes.[13]

So the living community, the life of faith, the sacred texts and the worshipping community are recognized as loci for revelation – and this includes the diversity of creation, as was discussed in Chapter 5. Catherine Hilkert points out that in beginning to develop a dialogical model of revelation, 'an increasing number of theologians ... would argue that in this dialogical model one cannot separate the revelation of God from the faith that perceives, receives, and responds to that offer' (p. 63). Thus, to be received, tradition needs an interpreting community, in fact, the *sensus fidelium*, the faithful witness and response of the whole people of God. Many would argue that the loss of the authority of the *sensus fidelium* is an important fact in the present crisis.

Once this is accepted, a window is opened to a relational understanding of tradition, rich in potential for the inclusion of the faith experience of all believing communities and open to the excluded voices across the centuries.[14] But this is still not a completely adequate starting-point, as it does not take into account how people are actually *using* the words 'tradition', 'revelation' and 'faith', and the emotional investment which they have in their own inter-pretation – which is deeply connected with the struggle to maintain identity, as I noted. As Tillard has written,

> Contained in my faith life today is the drama of Israel, the fruit of costly discussions at Nicaea and Chalcedon, what Francis of Assisi brought to fruition concerning the secrets of apostolic poverty, what thousands of unknown believers have testified as to the hope in their answers to their persecutors.[15]

The fact that he does not include the experience and witness of women, in a book which explores the nature of the Church as *communion*, is again an indicator that what still determines the canons of tradition and revelation is restricted to a small élite group. In many cases there is a stated *commitment* to dialogue and inclusivity without any idea as to the costly effort and change of consciousness necessary to make this work.

So to move forward I use the four meanings of tradition defined by Letty Russell, which are themselves building on the distinctions of the World Council Faith and Order Document of 1963.[16] The first category 'recognizes that all the distinctions are seeking to make clear the ways that the Church continues to stay connected to "The Tradition" as the action of God's mission in sending or handing over Jesus Christ to the world' (p. 37). Letty Russell then invents a second category, that of Scripture and Church doctrine, because this is one of the most frequent ways of referring to tradition. The third category is the process itself of handing over as it takes place in different cultures, contexts and communities. By naming this 'traditioning' in other words as an activity, its relational and ongoing character is emphasized. The fourth category is that of the different confessional 'traditions' or patterns of Church life. In practice, we encounter these different understandings of tradition as interwoven. It was an interweaving of this fourth strand, the prohibition against images as a pattern of life, with the second strand of doctrine as tradition ('Thou shalt not make graven images'), and with the active use of this as defining community identity (the third strand of traditioning), which caused the crisis for Asher Lev within Hasidic Judaism. Within Catholicism, many people still choose to receive communion on the tongue, even if this is no longer the rule, or confessional pattern (category 4), because it reinforces the security of the identity given by pre-Vatican II faith. It makes no difference to point out that Jesus broke and gave the bread with his hands at the Last Supper: tradition is far more complex than mere fidelity to what Jesus did!

But by emphasizing the active carrying forward of tradition into the future – the activity of traditioning (category 3) – feminist theologians together with other liberation theologians are able to understand the Church not merely as symbol of patriarchal domination, but as the bearer of 'transforming memory', a liberating memory with the power to transform the future from the present. The activity of reclaiming, proclaiming and creatively actualizing forgotten women and men, movements, traditions and texts, in regional, national and international networks, is already staggering and it is done in the name of, and in solidarity with, *authentic ecclesia*. Already there is a substantial body of work done by Rosemary Ruether, Elisabeth Fiorenza and Letty Russell[17] in creatively engaging with tradition. But because feminist theologians often, understandably, have distrusted institutional Church because of their continued exclusion from ministry and decision-making structures, and because of the abuse of power, the potential of liberating memory which is at the very heart of *ecclesia* is often under-used as a resource. We pay lip-service to eucharistic memory, or anamnesis, with little awareness of its cutting edge, its origins in the movement from oppression to freedom. In the last twenty years, Metz's idea of 'dangerous memory' has been developed by many liberation theologies as the memory both of freedom and of suffering and oppression.[18] Far too little attention is paid to the question of *who is doing the remembering*. For those who are silent and excluded, it is not so much a question of remembering, but how to live with the painful memories. I write now in Eastern Europe, having just visited the Jewish

Quarter of Prague. There I saw an exhibition of children's drawing from the camp at Theresienstadt, tragic, and at the same time overwhelmingly moving in the depiction of symbols of hope and joy. There can be no question of forgetting such tragedies and trauma. But can the communities and governments which inflicted such injustice and trauma on the scale of genocide enter into the kind of remembering which cannot change what has happened, but can work towards ensuring that it will not happen again? If the activity of *traditioning* included the consciousness that within *ecclesia* there are radically different sorts of memory, and different forms of *remembering* to be undergone, then new resources are made accessible. And our eucharistic communities rediscover their authentic roots.

As Charles Elliott described it in his recent book *Memory and Salvation*, there are four dimensions to the power of memory as it resides in ecclesia.[19] The first is Church as community of memories in the sense of being the accumulation of all expressions of being *ecclesia*, as described earlier. The second is the acting out or representation of these foundational memories in ritual, song, dance and, I would add, in symbol and architecture. Thus, when Lucy de Souza, in 'Biblical Women', the Hunger Cloth she designed for Misereor,[20] remembered Miriam leading her sisters in the dance (Exodus 3), she contextualized this in the drought situation in Rajasthan, India. Pharaoh in this context is the oppression of women having no water and being forced to walk across the desert in search of it; freedom means flowing water. Reclaiming the memory of Miriam in continuity with the biblical tradition (see Chapter 4) is at the same time remembering her for a new context.

The third type of remembering is what Elliott calls archetypal memory – with a substance to be mined which is deeper than all representations. He gives examples such as the archetypal symbols of *wounded healer, scapegoat, Mother Church, symbols of transcendence*, warning that these may have become detached from the wider, secular society. But it is precisely here that feminist theologians have been particularly active in pointing out the effect of these so-called archetypal symbols on vulnerable people, who are made into scapegoats or sacrificial victims. It is here that feminist theology acts as critical conscience against the universalizing of archetypal memory and its distancing from the lived experience of ordinary people.

Elliott's fourth type of remembering is the most deeply problematic. It refers to the debate about who has the right to interpret the Church's memory – the magisterium, the theologians, or the simple faith of ordinary people. In this, the *Dark Night of the Church*, the question is whether the magisterium has the humility to listen to the voices from the margins. Is it still possible, at this late stage, to give credence to other sources of authority? As the opening quotation to this chapter stated, feminist theologians, together with numerous groups loyal to the Vatican II vision of Roman Catholic Church, have a double commitment – to Christianity and universal Church, as well as to the well-being of all human beings and living creatures. Can a more organic and dynamic view of traditioning as a charge for the whole people of God find new ways forward?

Dipping into Miriam's Well: creative ways forward

Using the image of Miriam's Well is itself creatively remembering an ancient tradition. For in the Jewish mystical tradition is preserved the memory of Miriam's Well, which sprang up in the desert when the women were almost dying of thirst.[21] Throughout history, not only did Miriam's Well continue to spring up when her children were in dire need, but it still continues to inspire contemporary women to develop empowering rituals and symbols. As one Jewish woman wrote:

> I have always felt that I am sitting at a well and that if it's deep and there is a way of dipping into it and other people have dipped into it before . . . That well is, I would say, the collective experience of Jewish women.[22]

For Jewish, Christian and Islamic women, the inspiration of Miriam the prophet is crucial, as the growing literature testifies.[23] But it is not simply a question of recovering what is lost or suppressed, nor of reclaiming a lost tradition to empower a new context – as was the case with Lucy de Souza's Hunger Cloth. As Matthew's Gospel tells us: 'Every scribe who becomes a disciple of the kingdom of heaven is like a householder who brings out from his storeroom things both new and old' (Matthew 13:52). What is old is drawn from Miriam's Well and remembered. What is new is that women, marginalized groups and basic communities are envisioning new meanings for Christian *ecclesia*, offering a way forward from androcentrism, misogyny and the rule of kyriarchy. This is the new exodus. That is why the traditioning activity cannot be purely remembering: the image is much closer to Jesus' calling for new wineskins (Matthew 9:16–17). The old tradition of quilting expresses this activity colourfully. It is both remembering and creating simultaneously. The new creation, far from being merely an assembly of motley patches, expresses solidarity with communities of struggle, past and present, remembers the suffering of poor and forgotten women, evokes something of the labour of women working together to bring forth something new, and is itself a representation of some of the central symbols of the Christian story.[24]

The old–new character of this traditioning was given an exhilarating historical expression at the European Women's Synod in Gmünden, Austria, in July 1996. 'Traditionally'(!) women have not been key players at Church synods – if they have been present at all. (The one exception to this seems to have been the action of St Hilda of Whitby who, if she did not actually convene the Synod, presided over the Abbey of Whitby when the Synod took place in 664: this was to settle the dispute between the Roman and Celtic factions about the date of Easter.) But in meeting at Gmünden, over 1,000 women from 35 European countries – and fourteen countries from other parts of the world – reclaimed the synodical process with a different meaning. *Synodos* in Greek can mean 'journeying with'; this assembly came together to build a common household in Europe based on principles of justice, truth, integrity and commitment to Gospel values. Community-building occurred in many ways – eating and celebrating together, as well as through many rituals, both 'traditional' and creative, and through a common commitment to resolutions concerning politics, economics and spirituality.[25] Respecting the discussions and decision-making processes of women is one way of beginning the long process of healing. Telling and retelling the sacred stories, freed from patriarchal androcentrism, means beginning to live from a new reality. Thus 'Dipping into the Well' had produced a synodical process which, it was hoped, will eventually lead to an international synod of solidarity.[26]

Secondly, the process of creatively responding to tradition is actually happening through the networking of the many groups whose commitment is to the poorest, most marginalized and most discriminated against in the world. It is this networking of Christian communities already referred to which gives the most powerful sign that *people are yearning for the recovery of participatory community*. What is most heartening is not merely the communities of solidarity which are being formed on both a local and a global basis, but the rooting of the inspiration in the most fundamental Gospel values, *the core of the traditum. Across the world prophetic marginal groups are in dialogue with each other*. If we can work together *in trust and love*, showing how the distortions of patriarchal rule have kept in being malfunctioning configurations of Church (and continue to do so), then *through us, God is fashioning authentic ecclesia*. If we can only show how new forms of power and decision-making embody Gospel values, this, too, is fashioning *ecclesia. For it is not a question of denying legitimate authority and the need for good governance, or of creating new centres of power*: rather it is attempting to be faithful to the liberating memory of Jesus – the *kenosis* of patriarchy and heart of relational *ecclesia* – who dis-enthroned the legitimacy of the dominant, and replaced it with an ethic of mutuality-in-love.

Thirdly, the radical newness of the message of the Kingdom was in fact one of the most ancient of the prophetic Jewish traditions, but expressed in a new context, to a people hungry for justice. This sameness-yet-newness carries on: though we are in solidarity with all forms of oppression, it is crucial to be aware of new forms. We find neither AIDS sufferers in the New Testament nor discrimination against lesbians. What we do find is the tradition of condemnation of injustice against the poorest of the poor, the ever-new categories of people on the scrapheap of society. This is the memory which sustains and creates ever-new forms of *koinonia*. Yes, we are called to be bearers of tradition – but of this prophetic tradition. From Miriam to Isaiah to Jesus of Nazareth, from Hilda of Whitby to Hildegarde of Bingen, from Francis of Assisi to Dorothy Day and Petra Kelly, from Felicitas and Perpetua of North Africa to Archbishop Romero of El Salvador, these prophets of *authentic ecclesia* are the memory which liberates us from the Dark Night, and they go before us calling us to build communities of integrity, 'until the dawn comes and the morning star rises in your minds' (2 Peter 1:19).

Notes

1 Mary Catherine Hilkert, 'Experience and tradition' in *Freeing Theology: The Essential of Theology in Feminist Perspective*, ed. Catherine Mowry LaCugna (HarperSanFrancisco, 1993), pp. 77–8.

2 Many would of course say that the move was not due to this issue alone. It seemed that the ordination issue was the catalyst, symptomatic of something deeper. What should not be skirted around is the concealed misogyny of many of these positions. This being said, the movement was not as great as had been anticipated. What has caused even more disturbance is the admission of some *married* Anglican priests to the Roman Catholic priesthood, thus throwing into prominence the admissibility of married priests and the questioning of the validity of enforced celibacy.

3 The documentation manifests an increasing defensiveness on this point, in reaction to what has been happening in the Church of England. See *Inter Insigniores* (1976); *Mulieris Dignitatem* (1988); *Catechism of the Catholic Church* (London: Geoffrey Chapman, 1994), pp. 353–4.

4 For a recent description of the loci of tradition in the Roman Catholic Church, see Avery Dulles, 'Faith and revelation' in *Systematic Theology: Roman Catholic Perspectives*, ed. Francis Fiorenza and John P. Galvin (Dublin: Gill and Macmillan, 1991), pp. 120–2.

5 Chaim Potok, *My Name Is Asher Lev* (New York: Heinemann, 1972).

6 The same point was made by the sociologist Mary Douglas about the Irish in England observing the Friday abstinence. See Mary Douglas, *Natural Symbols: Explorations in Cosmology* (Harmondsworth: Penguin, 1978).

7 Elisabeth Behr-Sigel, *The Ministry of Women in the Church* (California: Oakwood, 1991), cited

in M. Grey, *The Wisdom of Fools?* (London: SPCK, 1993), p. 93.

8 T. S. Eliot, *East Coker* V, 23 in *The Four Quartets* (London: Faber and Faber, 1944).

9 The phrase is Letty Russell's: see *Feminist Interpretation of the Bible* (Philadelphia: Westminster, 1985).

10 See Dolores Williams, *Sisters in the Wilderness* (Maryknoll: Orbis, 1993); Elsa Tamez, 'The woman who complicated the history of salvation' in John Pobee and Bårbel Wartenburg-Potter, *New Eyes for Reading* (Geneva: WCC, 1986), pp. 3–17; Phyllis Trible, 'The desolation of rejection' in *Texts of Terror* (Philadelphia: Fortress, 1984), pp. 9–35.

11 For Women-Church, see M. Grey, *The Wisdom of Fools?*, ch. 9, pp. 120–36; Rosemary Radford Ruether, *Women-Church, Theology and Practice* (New York: Harper and Row, 1985); Mary-Jo Weaver, *New Catholic Women: A Contemporary Challenge to Contemporary Religious Authority* (San Francisco: Harper and Row, 1985).

12 See Phyllis Trible, *Texts of Terror*, pp. 65–91.

13 Cited in Mary Catherine Hilkert, 'Experience and tradition', p. 69.

14 It was just such an understanding of revelation which I explored in *The Wisdom of Fools?*

15 J.-M. R. Tillard, *Church of Churches: The Ecclesiology of Communion* (Collegeville, MN: Michael Glazier, 1992), p. 143, cited in Charles Elliott, *Memory and Salvation* (London: Darton, Longman and Todd, 1995), p. 221.

16 Letty Russell, *Church in the Round: A Feminist Interpretation of Church* (Louisville, KY: Westminster John Knox, 1993), ch. 1. This definition is itself an expansion of the 1963 Faith and Order study of the World Council of Churches. This distinguishes between 'The Tradition' which refers to Christ as the content of the traditioning process by which God hands over Christ to coming generations. 'The total traditioning process that operates in human history is called "tradition", and "traditions" is used for patterns of Church life such as confessions, liturgies' (p. 37).

17 For Ruether, see *Sexism and God-Talk: Towards a Feminist Theology* (London: SCM, 1983); for Fiorenza, see *Bread Not Stone: The Challenge of Biblical Interpretation* (Boston: Beacon, 1984); for Russell, in addition to *Church in the Round*, see *Household of Freedom: Authority in Feminist Theology* (Philadelphia: Westminster, 1987).

18 For dangerous memory in feminist theology see Elisabeth Schüssler Fiorenza, *In Memory of Her* (London: SCM, 1980); Sharon Welch, *Communities of Resistance and Solidarity* (Maryknoll: Orbis, 1985) M. Grey, *Redeeming the Dream* (London: SPCK, 1989); M. Grey, 'Liberation theology and the bearers of dangerous memory', *New Blackfriars* (May 1994).

19 Elliott, *Memory and Salvation*, pp. 221–5.

20 This Hunger Cloth, an inspiration for many liturgies of Women-Church, is also distributed by CAFOD and Christian Aid.

21 See Peruna V. Adelman, 'A drink from Miriam's cup: invention of tradition among Jewish women', *Journal of Feminist Studies in Religion* 10.2 (Fall 1994), pp. 151–66.

22 Ibid., p. 153.

23 For example, Catharina Halkes, *Met Miriam is alles Begonnen* (Baarn: Ten Have, 1980); Eleanor Broner, *The Telling* (HarperSanFrancisco, 1993); Elisabeth Moltmann-Wendel, Heidemarie Langer and Herta Leistner, *Met Miriam door de Rietzee* (Stuttgart, 1983; Boxtel, 1985); M. Grey, 'Empowered to lead: Sophia's daughters blaze a trail', keynote speech, Women's Synod, Gmünden, Austria (1996).

24 Letty Russell relates movingly of being given a quilt for her sixtieth birthday: 'The sisters who sat together and quilted the front have all graduated, but they and the others are not

forgotten. The back is covered with the names of many alumnae who are on that journey of choosing to become a woman ... for me, to look at the names is a form of what Toni Morrison called "Re-memory". It evokes pictures of life and patterns of relationships in a way similar to the powerful panels in the AIDS quilt': *Church in the Round*, p. 82.

25 See the *Documentation* of the Synod: Gertraud Lauer and Michaela Moser (eds), *Frauen bewegen Europa: Die Erste Europäische Frauensynode: Anstösse zur Veränderung* (Vienna and Munich: Verlagshaus Thaur, 1997).

26 The metaphor of the Well was used at the Synod both by Anna Karin Hammar in her keynote speech on 'Spirituality' and by myself in the keynote speech 'Empowered to lead'.

7

TRANSFORMING

O God our loving Eternal Parent, we praise you with a great shout of joy! Your ruling power has proved victorious! For centuries our land seemed too dark for sunrise, too bloody for healing, too sick for recovery, too hateful for reconciliation. But you have brought us into the daylight of liberation; you have healed us with new hope; you have stirred us to believe our nation can be reborn; we see the eyes of our sisters and brother shining with resolve to build a new South Africa. Accept our prayers of thanksgiving.

(Desmond Tutu[1])

I came to cast fire on the earth; and would that it were already kindled!

(Luke 12:49)

The euphoria at the end of apartheid in South Africa and the prominent part played by Archbishop Tutu and other Church leaders highlights what this chapter is about – namely, transformation. In a nutshell, transformation of self and world. Transformation of diseased patterns of relating between persons and governments nationally and internationally. Transformation of systems of interaction based on militarism, on racial hatred, of all rules of domination. Never has the Church claimed to exist for itself, and to be a self-enclosed, self-congratulating community, committed solely to ensuring eternal life for its obedient members. The Constitution of Vatican II *Lumen Gentium* proclaimed what has always been the insight of authentic *ecclesia*, to exist not for itself but to be a light for the nations (Isaiah 42:6; 49:6) for the *turning around of the evil systems which hold societies in thrall*. For *authentic revolution,* or the bringing about of the *nova res*, through the proclamation of the values of the Kingdom of God. To encounter the earthly Jesus was to be transformed, to live to different values, different dreams, to live out of a constantly renewable source of hope. Throughout history the experience of *authentic* conversion – rather than enforced proselytism, or the many varieties of *cuius regio, eius religio* – has brought a heady experience of being changed, followed by a deepening sense of

91

faith, committed to personal conversion, and to the transformation of immediate community and the wider world.

Transforming society in the name of the ethics of the Kingdom, through its witness to truth and justice, is the most cherished part of the Church's mission, never totally lost sight of and always glimpsed in new forms. Before and during the fall of communism in 1989, it was the Church's prophetic role which sustained hope in the people. Candle-lit vigils in the churches of the former East Germany and Czechoslovakia witness to this. The murder, in November 1989, of the six Jesuits in El Salvador with their housekeeper and her daughter was another reminder that the prophetic stance for justice for the poor taken by the murdered Archbishop Romero in that country was not only dynamically alive, but *deeply ecclesial* in nature: the murdered Jesuits' actions in the name of truth, were actions of the Church of the poor: 'This world which gives death to so many millions of people also lies about it. It tries to ignore death very consciously; even worse, it uses euphemisms to cover death up.'[2] *Transformation* from a culture which is death-dealing, and unable to speak the truth, to a different value system, must be at the heart of the ethics of the 'beloved community'. It is constantly emphasized by Jesus: yet too often the call to conversion (Mark 1:14), to love and forgive our neighbour, is understood minimally, in a privatized way. Indeed, it could hardly be otherwise, given the current narcissistic individualism and lack of a community-based spirituality.

Yet it was precisely within a community that Jesus' love ethic was to be embodied. The beloved community was to be as a city on a mountain top, a light to the nations, the light set firmly on a stand (Luke 11:33; Matthew 5:13–16), the salt of the earth, the new Jerusalem, the Messianic banquet where the poor and marginalized were the honoured guests (Luke 14:16–24), the tree which offered shelter to all the birds of the air (Luke 13:18–19), the community where the gifts and ministries of all were needed, a place of proclamation of Kingdom values.

How, then, is it possible to recover the urgency of *transforming* world as a dimension of Church? This chapter tries to lay the foundations for the *ethics of the beloved community*[3] in order to recall the Church to the challenge of world transformation as the fundamental core of authentic *ecclesia*.

A passion for justice-making

The ethics of the beloved community[4] are energized by the same fire which Jesus wanted to kindle on the earth. This was the same fire sent earlier upon the prophet Jeremiah (Lamentations 1:13). I am convinced that it was also the same fire with which the prophet Miriam found the courage to be a leader among her people even before the children of Israel fled Pharaoh. The fires of passion and compassion are always the fuel for communities of resistance and solidarity-in-justice.[5] And this fire is not a fantasy! Many contemporary Christians have been empowered and energized by, for example, creative liturgies of the Women-Church movement, celebrations of commitment within the many Peace groups and Justice and Peace movements, and from earth-based rituals celebrating creation. Some of these liturgies have been in the name of the official Church – many not. Some have witnessed to an ecumenical and interfaith relation not yet possible through official channels. Such is the way the prophetic Spirit has worked through history: without the passion for justice which will not be quenched, the daring to witness to a deeper truth – that God loves *all* people and longs for that interconnection and just relating between all which will bring transformation and real community – there would be no movement to unity. Stasis and boredom with the issue would prevail. Of course, ecumenism and interfaith agreements must continue at an official level: but without the grassroots passion for relating, and commitment to understanding each other's experiences and sacred stories, ecumenism is in danger of becoming a question of argument about propositions, far removed from living as the community which knows itself beloved. At this juncture in history, when, in the recent war in Bosnia, *Christian* soldiers have raped thousands of Bosnian *Muslim* women,[6] it is time to bring a *passion for right relating* upmost in our ethical ecumenical discourse. The nettle must be grasped. Ways forward are both immensely complex and at the same time very simple. For example, at the European Women's Synod in Gmünden (already referred to), Muslim women present asked that every time the word 'Church' was mentioned in our resolutions, that it was substituted by 'faith community', which would include them. What a small thing to do in terms of solidarity-in-faith! After I had given a lecture in terms of the role of Sophia in the Bible as a model for the leadership of women, one Muslim participant shyly asked me if I would think of including the role of Fatima (daughter of Muhammad), as also inspirational: she meant so much for Muslim women and functioned in the same way as Sophia does for the Jewish and Christian faiths. Again, what a small thing to do ...

Yet the passion for justice-making which is at the heart of the process of transformation is of its essence *counter-cultural*. So has it ever been with movements of transformation, as Jeremiah, Buddha, Jesus, Francis of Assisi, Catherine of Siena and many of the great foundresses of religious congregations have discovered. There never has been a great and enduring *spirituality* which has not been counter-cultural in challenging the ethos of the times. But too often the *ethics* of Christian community have made alliances compromising with and even stimulating the deadly systems of violence which dominate so-called civilization. Crusades, witchhunts, pogroms, the Inquisition and the corrupt lifestyle of former popes are obvious historical examples. But the recent examples of the involvement of the Church with the downfall of the Sandinista government in Nicaragua, and the continued suppression of the movements for liberation among the poor of Latin America, together with the silencing of the theologians who support them, calls into question the authenticity of the Church as the *Church of the poor with a genuine option for the poor*. This is one of the greatest sources of scandal to young people, my own children included – and one of the reasons why they are leaving the Church in droves. (This is not to doubt that the Church is faithful to concern for the poor in many ways; and to affirm that concerted action against racism, homelessness and on behalf of asylum-seekers must be applauded and encouraged.) To recall again the plea of Rodolfo Cardenal cited in Chapter 1: the *culture of simplicity* which he called for, to transform the lives of the *crucified peoples*: this is the hope and commitment of liberation theology and all kinds of liberation theologians, a commitment, in the name of the crucified and risen Christ, to permeate and transform the ethics of violence and domination.

It is the image of the woman with the measure of yeast (Luke 13:20) with which all the meal was leavened, as image of the Kingdom of God, which brings hope.[7] It is this very permeation of the *passion for just relating* which functions as transformative yeast. This is the transformative yeast which activates the energies of the basic communities – yes, in Latin and Central America, but also in Europe and all parts of the globe, where contextual forms of basic ecclesial communities (such as Women-Church) re-invent the Church, to use Leonardo Boff's telling phrase.[8] It is a passion which will not be stilled or quenched.

And the challenge today is to be counter-cultural in challenging the killing systems of violence, and yet not to be *anti-world*. The challenge is not to discover that the world is evil, and so transform the Church into a sect, which defines itself *over against* the world – as has happened many times in the past: what is needed is to see, in the many secular developments, new possibilities for Church and faith communities. It is a tragic irony that just at the time of the most serious environmental crisis, at a time when the latest statistics on world poverty show how much poorer the poor of the world have become,[9] from the various angles of new cosmology, creation spirituality and theology as well as the work of feminist philosophers,[10] a holistic re-valuing of creation and appreciation of the divine in creation is inspiring faith communities and secular groups alike.[11] This is mirrored by the alliances working for peace and non-violence, again within and without the faith communities. Both CND and Pax Christi International (a Church organization) have reorganized strategies since the removal of the Cruise weapons from Greenham Common; the focus has become much more directed to both the legitimacy of conventional weapons and warfare, and the need to build a culture of peace. But my point here is that the attraction to these groups is wider than official Church membership. The same point can be made for the struggle against racism and the efforts of the gay and lesbian communities to fight for acceptance and just treatment.

Could this be the kairos moment for a new understanding of the nature of Church – poised as we are on the fulcrum between valuing the discipleship and community of Church, with her long commitment to promoting the fullness of humanity, the protection of innocent life in all forms, and yet the reality that many justice movements are wider than Church but not unrelated to it? I now explore this kairos moment in three different ways.

Church, enabler of many communities?

Fragmentation, loss of community, individualism, and the turmoil following the fall of communism in Central and Eastern European countries all seem to give even more urgency to the Church functioning as *transforming leaven* – but call for a variety of new and different ways. That there remains a culture of fear in many of these countries is sadly manifest. Communism may have been toppled, but its ghost lurks in many ways, not least in the terror which people feel against speaking out and telling the real truth of their lives. In countries like Hungary and the Czech Republic where for the last fifty years the Church has lived through and supported a culture of resistance against communism, or in highly-secularized countries where young people have lost familiarity with religious traditions, it is not the methods of brash evangelism which will make the Church the real leaven for society's transformation, but the supporting and enabling of communities of justice and solidarity, and the many connections between them. *The challenge is to support and enable the many ways of being Church.* Truth is risky, love is even more risky and it is much easier to create than to heal divisions – as the ecumenical movement knows, all too painfully. In the fragmented climate of postmodern culture, the redeeming task of *gathering the fragments* must be the truly ecclesial one. Could this be the way in which a new dawn for the Church is being ushered in?

Yet it is vital to understand, respect and uphold contextuality. In the context of Eastern and Central Europe, to begin with, where, until recently, repression came from the state, reading the Bible and worshipping openly now represent a freedom which 'progressive' Western Christianity finds hard to appreciate. There can be a pride in being *openly* Christian which the West finds strange. Again, the critical manner with which feminist theologians reread the Bible in order to uncover liberating perspectives can seem alien when looked at from the perspective of the East. Furthermore, to Third World theologians, for whom the Bible sustains the struggle for survival and justice, the Western feminist theological critique of sacrifice, and the stress laid on self-affirmation, can seem like indulgence. How can *authentic ecclesia* hold together these extremes – and many more? The Women-Church movement has given a clear example of this need to be open to apparently conflicting perspectives.[12] For the emphasis placed on listening to stories, hearing into speech and providing safe spaces of mutual trust for this to take place is no arbitrary activity: it is in fact recontextualizing the days of persecution of the early Christians, the dangerous narratives of resistance and suffering, at a time when women still do suffer violence and poverty – and do not experience institutional Church as a safe space from which to speak out. But it is also making spaces for articulating differences and for the beginning of the healing of the deep divisions between women themselves, be these of race, economic gulf, sexuality, faith community or life-experience.

Secondly, a great challenge for *ecclesia* is to shed the defensive attitude, the boundaries between what is to count as sacred sources of inspiration and what is not. With a renewed understanding of revelation and tradition (Chapter 6), and with the humility which recognizes that God's truth includes the whole of creation, a new openness becomes possible. Rosemary Ruether set out a framework for inspirational sources of theology in using five strands: ancient Near Eastern texts and Graeco-Roman religion; the prophetic/heretical sects of early Christianity – like Gnostics or Montanists, as well as prophetic groups and movements throughout history, for example, the Shakers and Quakers; Scripture, both Hebrew and Christian; critical post-Christian world-views; and, of course, the basic concepts of the traditional theological system itself – creation/redemption/eschatology – suitably re-envisioned.[13] With a confidence in the omnipresence of the Holy Spirit, who weaves in and out of all faiths, there are many ways of being enriched by each other's traditions. Gandhi listened to a part of the New Testament every day. And there are rich resources from Gandhi's own vision which could help reconcile Christian tensions between personal and social liberation.[14] Such an openness would facilitate understanding between those Christians who find the Bible their only source of faith inspiration, those from global contexts where Christianity represents a small minority (for example in Asia), and those whose sacred texts are wholly secular.

We would be enabled to see that when Chung Hyun Kyung, the charismatic Korean feminist theologian, appeals to Buddhism, shamanism, feminism *and* Christianity, this does not represent a watering-down of Christian tradition but the exploration of more enriching possibilities through entering into relation with all these traditions.[15] It would be possible to understand that dialoguing with the Goddess movement is not a betrayal of the God of Christianity, but a way of appreciating how Christianity could learn from the earth wisdom which is honoured in the rituals and life-style of the many forms of this movement.[16]

When seen from the perspective of transformation, the praxis of authentic *ecclesia* is all important. This, the praxis of right relation, is based on an ethics of connection.[17] To replace an ethics of domination, isolation and separation, and transform a society based on these, an ethics of connection flows from a relational world-view. Understanding humanity and all living entities as fundamentally interdependent,[18] an ethics of connection resists any interpretation which privileges one section of humanity over another, any structure which blocks right relation and thus any form of community which embodies wrong, unjust or exploitative relation, injurious to humanity and creation alike. Connection respects diversity and is always yearning for authentic embodied relation where the dualistic splits between emotion and action, heart, mind and body are reconciled.

If the Church is understood as the enabler and sustainer of right relation in community, what this could mean practically is that she discerns and proclaims where community embodies the values of the Kingdom. Concretely, to take first the dimension of *dwelling* (Chapter 5), the Church can transform by becoming and allying herself with sustainable communities. Alvin Pitcher, in *Listen to the Crying of the Earth*, speaks of *nurturing connectedness* as the major function of many Christian Churches.[19] It was the praxis of this right relation which led the Churches to be committed to the programme 'Justice, Peace and Integrity of Creation'.[20] Much of the literature produced by this, and many Church efforts to recycle – for life-style communities are all worthwhile embodiments of the praxis of right relation as regards the earth – are to be encouraged. My point here is that they do not go far enough. *Ecclesia* as enabler of just community has to work to nurture connectedness and right relation with, for example, environmental pressure groups, politicians and industrial consortia. Simply because we are working in the name of Kingdom values we have a voice for the earth – which is voiceless – which no one else can articulate. But as yet we will not be respected as such. There is an enormous amount of groundwork – literally – to be done, to redeem the legacy of the misappropriated theological traditions with regard to the earth. As long as people can read the creation stories of Genesis as licence to dominate and exploit the earth, the Church's voice is not effective. Hence the need to work humbly with all *friends of the earth* – before it is too late.

Secondly, the praxis of the ethics of connection can draw on the very tradition of care and hospitality for which the Church has stood across the centuries. In fact, Letty Russell has written a whole theology of Church, calling on the core notion of hospitality as inspiration for justice-making.[21] Hospitality is a cherished tradition in the sense of welcoming the homeless and the stranger:

> I saw a stranger yestreen
> I put food in the eating place
> Drink in the drinking place
> For oft, oft goes the Christ in the stranger's guise
> For oft, oft, oft goes the Christ in the stranger's guise.[22]

But hospitality has even deeper roots. It is a grounding notion of human community. It evokes the hospitality of the earth, on whose graciousness we depend for every breath we draw. It is also, ultimately, the hospitality of God. It is into this hospitality that we make our final journey, our homecoming into God.[23]

But we can also draw on the notion of hospitality, care and communion to make new connections. In other words, to care for each other across and beyond the traditional boundaries of Church. The need to stem the flood of violence, to care for the earth, to tackle world hunger and the refugee problems are the problems for *all* humanity. It is time to break down the barriers and for *authentic ecclesia* to work much more genuinely with Muslims, Hindus, Sikhs and Buddhists, with African tribal religions, with indigenous Indians – and with people of no religious faith. In her moving book *Encountering God*, the Harvard Professor of Comparative Religion, Diana Eck, spoke of the gifts of hospitality she received from Hinduism on her many visits to India.[24] This was a hospitality where she felt drawn by the Hindu understanding of Spirit, of incarnation – and went back to her Christian roots enriched. There is a hunger for recovery of the sacred coming from unexpected quarters, a hunger for communion across the divisions. The Peace groups, Amnesty International, life-style groups, are but a few witnesses to this. The role which Bishop Desmond Tutu played in South Africa, the prophetic role of the Church in achieving the downfall of communism – these are the tangible signs giving grounds for hope that the Church is able to work humbly with non-religious groups.

Thirdly, she is able to do this because she draws deeply on her roots in reconciling/liberating. The sources of Hebrew and Christian Scriptures all speak of a new heart, a new spirit (Ezekiel 36), of new wine, new wineskins and of new creation. In some way the transformation process must break the cycle of victim/oppressor, of domination/submission. The problem is that the language of *swords into ploughshares* has somehow become so familiar that it has lost its power to transform our consciousness today. What can it mean when we read, day after day, of little girls kept imprisoned in cellars to be raped, prostituted, and finally starved to death?[25] (A phenomenon of both First and Third Worlds.) Mandela – as the introductory quotation to this chapter shows – lit a candle of hope when, in creating the new constitution of South Africa, he offered the path of reconciliation instead of the expected bloodbath of black against white. There is a strong argument that the true Christian path is that of non-violence, and the Quaker and Mennonite traditions are faithful witnesses to this.[26]

Transforming – the complete changing of shape of society – is the goal. A complete revolution of consciousness – no less – is what is aimed for. *Authentic ecclesia* has in her very being the *language* of urgency, the *energy* to sustain action, the *passion* for justice, praxis and transformation of inner and outer selves, the *authority* to change the patterns through which we relate. The face of the humiliated Christ is still manifest in the rejected of society – and now especially in the abused and murdered children. They may be close to the angels of heaven, as Jesus said, but this society has created for them a living hell. Reconciliation and liberation are two sides of the same coin: liberation, the actual experience of freedom and justice, is the fruit of the process of reconciliation. Reconciliation is the gift of the victim or the wronged. It can never be forced upon the victim by the command to forgive – which is frequently an abuse of power, truth and justice. This is where the work of theologians, conflict mediation experts, feminist counsellors of rape victims can work together,[27] showing how transformation is built from taking small steps for change, from never giving way to becoming locked into bitterness, revenge and despair, but always respecting the parameters of justice.

But the passion for transformation, the longing for the embodiment of the Kingdom, will not be sustained without the fifth dimension of *ecclesia*, the dimension of *vision*. It is to this that I now turn.

Notes

1 Cited in Jim Wallis, *The Soul of Politics* (San Diego: Harcourt Brace and Co., 1994), p. 297. He is describing the historic scene in the stadium at the 1994 elections, just before the speech of Mandela, which offered reconciliation instead of a bloodbath.

2 Jon Sobrino, 'The greatest love', interview with Jim Wallis, *Sojourners* 19.3 (April 1990), pp. 16–18.

3 Later chapters develop the dimensions of spirituality and life-style which underpin the ethical.

4 'The beloved community' is the phrase of Martin Luther King. It has fired the imagination of many writers. See M. Grey, 'From patriarchy to beloved community: exploring new models of ministry for feminist theology', *Feminist Theology* 3 (May 1993). I use the phrase deliberately here to evoke the different nature of relating to which genuine Christian community invites.

5 See Mercy Oduyoye and Virginia Fabella (eds), *With Passion and Compassion* (Maryknoll: Orbis, 1985).

6 Clearly, this is a complex issue, which should not be dealt with lightly. The statistics of exactly how many of the raped women were Christian and how many were Muslim are hard to find. We researched these carefully for the EATWOT dialogue among women theologians from South and North (December 1994 in Costa Rica) concerning violence against women. See *Proceedings of the Dialogue*, European Report. Also, the book which issued from it: *Women Resisting Violence* (Maryknoll: Orbis, 1996), ed. M. Mananzan, M. Oduyoye, E. Tamez, A. Clarkson, M. Grey and L. Russell. It must be said that the full ethical implications as to the way Christians treated Muslims have not yet been tackled.

7 This is the central image of the Hunger Cloth (Hünger Tuch) of Lucy de Souza, mentioned in Chapter 6. Again it is contextualized in an Indian context, as the woman is encased in an ear of corn, which is depicted as a mandala.

8 Leonardo Boff, *Ecclesio-Genesis: Basic Communities Re-invent the Church* (Brazil, 1977; Maryknoll: Orbis, 1986).

9 'The Rich, they will always be with us. But never in the history of the world have they been present in such quantities and in such flamboyant contrast with the poor as now. The year's most halting statistic has come in the UN's new Human Development Report. Take it in slowly: the total wealth of the world's 358 billionaires equals the combined incomes of the poorest 45 per cent of the world's population – 2.3 billion people': 'Highway robbery by the super-rich', *The Guardian* (22 July 1996).

10 An example of this would be Val Plumwood, *Feminism and the Mastery of Nature* (London: Routledge, 1993). The overcoming of the radical dualisms which have damaged women and nature alike in the Western philosophical tradition has created new possibilities for healing, just and holistic relations between women, men and nature.

11 Creation spirituality, which has been associated with Matthew Fox (see *Original Blessing: A Primer in Creation Spirituality* (Santa Fe: Bear and Co., 1981)), has now inspired numerous groups, both with Church affiliations and beyond or outside, to come together for rituals celebrating the earth, to rediscover ancient wisdom cosmologies and to form alternative life-style groups. See the work of the Creation Spirituality Centre at St James's, Piccadilly, London.

12 See M. Grey, *The Wisdom of Fools?* (London: SPCK, 1993), ch. 9.

13 See Rosemary Radford Ruether, *Sexism and God-Talk* (London: SCM, 1983).

14 For example, John Chathanatt SJ, at the 'Liberating the Vision' Summer School (LSU College, 1996), showed how Gandhi's idea of *swaraj*, freedom, moved from being personal discipline to incorporating a wider vision of liberation and justice for the poorest of people. See *Proceedings of the Summer School* (LSU, 1996).

15 See Chung Hyun Kyung's sermon 'Come, Holy Spirit' at Canberra, the WCC Conference, as well as *Struggle To Be the Sun Again* (Maryknoll: Orbis, 1993).

16 It is clear that not all forms of the Goddess movement offer the same potential. My own position is neither to agree with the hypothesis of 'the golden age of the goddess' (because this is simply unhistorical), nor to the reclaiming of Goddesses like Aphrodite for the present (as does Carol Christ, *The Laughter of Aphrodite: Reflections on a Journey to the Goddess* (San Francisco: Harper and Row, 1987)), as again, this seems an act of illusory wishful thinking, culturally misplaced; but to listen and learn what it means for God to be female, and to understand the significance of the values and wisdom involved. See the critique of Rosemary Ruether, *Gaia and God* (New York: HarperCollins, 1993), ch. 6.

17 For the ethics of connection, see M. Grey, *The Wisdom of Fools?*, ch. 4; 'Claiming power-in-relation – but with whom?', *Journal of Feminist Studies in Religion* 7.1 (April 1994), pp. 7–15.

18 See my arguments in *Redeeming the Dream* (London: SPCK, 1989).

19 Alvin Pitcher, *Listen to the Crying of the Earth: Cultivating Creation Communities* (Cleveland: The Pilgrim Press, 1993), p. 95.

20 Although this has produced a great amount of literature, sadly it has not had anything like the effect hoped for in concrete actions and commitment of the Churches to making environmental concerns a priority. See Chapter 5.

21 Letty Russell, *Church in the Round: A Feminist Interpretation of Church* (Louisville, KY: Westminster John Knox, 1993).

22 The source is an old Gaelic saying, recovered by Kenneth McCleod. Of course this notion is not confined to Celtic Christianity. It is much more of a reality in the poorer communities of Asia and Africa than it is in the affluence of Western Europe and North America.

23 See Nelle Morton, *The Journey Is Home* (Boston: Beacon, 1986).

24 Diana Eck, *Encountering God* (London: SPCK, 1995).

25 *The Guardian* (21 August 1996).

26 See, for example, John Dear, *The God of Peace: Toward a Theology of Non-Violence* (Maryknoll: Orbis, 1994).

27 See Marie Fortune, *Sexual Violence: The Unmentionable Sin* (New York: Pilgrim, 1983).

8

DREAMING

And the Lord answered me:
'Write the vision;
make it plain upon tablets,
so he may run who reads it.
For still the vision awaits its time;
it hastens to the end – it will not lie.
If it seem slow, wait for it;
it will surely come, it will not delay.'

(Habakkuk 2:2–3)

When warm weather came, Baby Suggs, holy, followed by every black man, woman and child who could make it through, took her great heart to the Clearing ... After situating herself on a huge, flat-sided rock, Baby Suggs bowed her head and prayed silently ... Then she shouted, 'Let the children come!' and they ran from the trees toward her.

'Let your mothers hear you laugh,' she told them, and the woods rang. The adults looked on and could not help smiling.

Then, 'Let the grown men come,' she shouted. They stepped out one by one from among the ringing trees.

'Let your wives and children see you dance,' she told them and groundlife shuddered under their feet.

Finally she called the women to her. 'Cry,' she told them, 'for the living and the dead. Just cry ... '

In the silence that followed, Baby Suggs, holy, offered to them her great big heart. She did not tell them to clean up their lives or go and sin no more. She did not tell them they were the blessed of the earth, its inheriting meek, or glorybound poor.

She told them that the only grace they could have was *the grace they could imagine. That if they did not see it, they would not have it* ... [My italics]

(Toni Morrison[1])

What sustains the journeying, the dwelling, traditioning and transforming processes or dimensions of *ecclesia*, is of course the power of vision. As Habakkuk says, we have to wait for it, to trust that it will come, and to believe that it brings its own rhythm, its own fulfilling potential. This chapter explores the power of envisioning or dreaming as the sustaining power of authentic *ecclesia*. It tries to reclaim the task of envisioning as one for the whole people of God. Not for a minute do I deny that there are those specially gifted and chosen for visions and revelations. Some of the most cherished jewels of the Christian tradition are the mystical gifts of Hildegarde, Julian of Norwich, John of the Cross and Teresa of Avila (among others). Here I try to do two things: to widen the concept of visioning to include the powers of imagination, dreaming and the energy of hoping; and secondly, to understanding this as a ministry and mission of the whole people of God.[2]

A bizarre feature of our society is that, to the degree that empiricism, death of soul, loss of spirituality and the triumph of secular values surround us, the language and discourse of dreams is common currency. But herein lies the danger. Not all that passes as *dream* has any remote connection with dreaming the Kingdom of God! Indeed, it could be said that *society is a bad dream from which we long to awake!* As I have been implying all through this book, it would seem that Disneyland and media extravaganzas have hijacked our dreams, replacing them with yearnings and longings which have nothing to do with the deepest and most genuine dimensions of humanity, namely with fantasies of luxury outside the reach of all but a few. Illusions of riches, daydreams of monetary success and fame create the false self, the soulless society, where only fragments of integrity remain. Ironically, nostalgia abounds for the lost dream – even if this is of a Golden Age which exists only in wishful thinking.

I want to show a different story. Media truth, TV fantasy, Disneyland allure is not all there is to it. If postmodern suspicion has value as method, then we can challenge the so-called universalism of the materialistic dream. This is the task of authentic *ecclesia* – which must then be empowered by a different dream. Once we take the activity of dreaming seriously, we discover we have wonderful *compañeras*, companions on this journey – within and outside the Churches. For years the Jungian psychoanalysts have been telling us to listen to our dreams. Have we not looked with envy upon shamanism within, for example, North American Indian spirituality, where the profundity of the dreams is the proof of the authentic shaman? Are there not countless communities witnessing to a different truth, protesting that *the way we are is not the way we have to be?* Just as, forty years ago, the children of the ghetto of Theresienstadt had drawn pictures of flowers, light and symbols of hope, so more recently, when the shells fell on the city of Sarajevo during the Bosnian war, the children hidden in the basements drew pictures of peace – their birds, flowers and butterflies imagined a different world.[3] Within Christian theology itself, the consciousness of the power of the dream acquired a recent awakening in the Sixties with Martin Luther King's speech 'I have a dream'. There followed a flurry of 'I have a dream' speeches: close on their heels was a genre of theological dream books,[4] from a variety of contexts as disparate as liberation or feminist theologies and ecologically inspired groups, as well as from more conventional sources.

It may be true that the recourse to dream is not free of ideological persuasion. Such is the heritage of dreams, their potential link with the transcendent, that to be able to back up an agenda with the authority of a dream is indeed a useful tool. But there is a world of difference when a politician claims credibility through the backing of a dream, and when authentic *ecclesia* does so: *ecclesia is faithful to God's great dream of the Kingdom of God.* It is to this dream that communities in solidarity with poor, oppressed and persecuted peoples are faithful. God's dream for creation as embodied in Christian faith and authentic *ecclesia* offers sustaining alternatives to society's bad dream. This is the *grace* that we have to grasp hold of with the power of imagination. It is offered, but vulnerable and fragile: Yeats's line 'tread softly, for you tread on my dreams' is all too relevant to the dream of the Kingdom/kin-dom of the vulnerable God.

Dreaming God's dream ...

To begin to speak about God's dream is to enter the imaginative discourse of symbols and metaphor which are best expressed in poetry, art and music: Carter Heyward expressed the dream out of which God created the universe as a longing for relationship:

> In the beginning was God,
> In the beginning the source of all that is,
> God yearning,
> God moaning,
> God labouring,
> God giving birth,
> God rejoicing,
> And God loved what she had made,
> And God said,
> 'It is good'.
> And God, knowing that all that is good is shared,

held the earth tenderly in her arms.
God yearned for relationship.
God longed to share the good earth,
And humanity was born in the yearning of God,
We were born to share the earth.
(From *Our Passion for Justice: Images of Power, Sexuality, and Liberation*
by Carter Heyward, copyright © 1984, The Pilgrim Press. Permission is
granted for this one-time use.)

What she described in terms of the yearning for relationship, the cosmologist
Brian Swimme sees in terms of the universe as a mystery of loving:

> The great mystery is that we are interested in anything whatever. Think of your
> friends, how you first met them, how interesting they appear to you. Why should
> anyone in the world interest us at all? Why don't we experience everyone as
> utter, unendurable bores? Why isn't the cosmos made that way? Why don't we
> suffer intolerable boredom with every person, forest, symphony and seashore in
> existence? The great surprise is that something or someone is interesting. Love
> begins there. Love begins when we discover interest. To be interested is when we
> fall in love. To become fascinated is to step into a wild love affair on any level
> of life.[5]

This great mystery of creation sustaining and being sustained in tenderness, of
yearning and loving relation, took a *particular* historical expression in the
covenanting between God and the children of Israel and, subsequently, through
Jesus' proclamation of the Kingdom of God. This *God of the dream* I have been
speaking of throughout as the power to make right and just relation, the power
to make the connections, the God in travail for the birthing of the Kingdom,
Sophia-God, Holy Wisdom, a God of *hospitality*.[6] This is the earthed dream out
of which *ecclesia* is the cherished – but erring – child. The grounding of the
dream in the life, ministry and praxis of Jesus of Nazareth remains normative
for Christian Church. That this normativeness is expressed in doctrine and
regulation is abundantly clear. That it is embodied in symbol – art, architecture
and music – is also beyond dispute. But there has been a tragic lack of awareness
that it also needs expression through the power of imagination and the power of
dreams – and that this level of expression is extremely vulnerable.

Imagination is one of the most neglected of theological tools, even if some
good philosophical reflection has been evoked in the last few years.[7] 'What we
are contending with is that the patriarchal/kyriarchal imagination has culmi-
nated in necrophilic or death-dealing ways of interrelating. If all we can imagine
are violent solutions to society's problems, hierarchical patters of relating,
confrontation as the way to solve conflicts, subordinating women and minority

groups in order to maintain law and order, severer punishments to curb criminality, *this is not merely a failure of ethics but one of imagination*. Imagination – the language of the psyche – remains diseased and stultified when imprisoned within the patriarchal order of domination and submission, and within all the oppressive dualisms which privilege those who hold power. *It is on the level of the dreaming, imagining and desiring psyche* (as was argued in Chapter 4, with the re-uniting of *psyche* and *eros*) *that the work of transforming patterns of relating begins to happen.*

The power of imagining, which issues from the wholeness of re-united *psyche* and *eros*, is neither disembodied rational activity nor egocentric wishful thinking. It refuses to divorce passionate caring from analysis, discernment or the need for action. This imagining springs from a qualitatively different perception, akin perhaps to the perception of the poet and to the attentiveness of the mystic. Adrian Hastings speaks of the need for the intertwining of passion and perception for prophecy:

> If we think back to creative visionaries like Blake, Dostoievski or Simone Weil, we can be both entranced and appalled by the power and consequences of their passion: so subtly perceptive in some things, so dangerously, madly, wrong in others. There seems a kind of spiritual and moral truth, immeasurably valuable, yet unattainable except through drinking of a chalice whose wine too easily spins dreams eschatological and wild. We would profoundly fail to interpret Jesus aright if we refused to locate him and his sayings in part within that almost mad wisdom where the human psyche experiences the divine at its most unsettling and contradictory and utopian.[8]

The visionary imagination, far from passively waiting for an angelic tap on the shoulder or the blinding Damascus flash,[9] is grounded historically in the flesh and blood way the dream of the Kingdom of God has been presented to us. The Beloved's vineyard (Isaiah 5), the wolf dwelling with the lamb (Isaiah 11), the holy mountain (Isaiah 25), water breaking forth in the wilderness (Isaiah 35:6b) – these were the ways in which the dream acquired its earthing, and these are but a few examples. Ecological dwelling in all its aspects is drawn into the urgency of the Kingdom of God. Jesus of Nazareth continued to put flesh on these bones, re-emphasizing that the blind would see, the lame walk and the poor have the good news preached to them (Matthew 11:5), that the lowliest had a privileged place (Luke 13:20) and that the Kingdom is not a reality for an imagined future but a reality to be grounded in the present (Luke 17:21). That there is not a fuller fleshing-out of the reality is not the point: it is like asking why the painter painted only this bit of the landscape, why Beethoven in his 'Pastoral' Symphony only depicted – musically – the shepherd boy's song after the storm. Jesus earthed the dream in the best way possible in his own context – *and he himself, who he was, was part of the earthing.*

In the Book of Revelation is seen the fullest earthed development of the dream of the Kingdom of God in the New Testament. John presents us the Church afflicted, in the extremity of near defeat by the powers of evil (the Beast). I sense a deeply rooted despair in what has become of *ecclesia* (Rev 1:4 – 3.22). All vision has vanished. Hence the rooting of the essence of *ecclesia* is in the vision of the presence and holiness of God, in direct continuity with the Hebrew Scriptures, and the mission of the Lamb to the earth (4 – 10). Once the powers of evil have been defeated, the vision of the new and redeemed creation is presented. The language is completely over the top – there is no need of sun or moon, so great is the glory of God (21:23). The first heaven and earth have passed away and the sea is no more (21:1).[10] But the message is clear. Here God is dwelling. Here is creation's home – not in some imagined, extraterrestrial paradise.

But if Jesus of Nazareth lived out the dream in a specific form, *Christ is the embodiment of power-in-relation.* Yet 'power-in-relation' is not confined to Christ. Healing, transforming power – as I have been arguing – springs from Messianic community, 'Christa community'. No one can dream our dreams of the kin-dom of right relations for us. Yes, our dreams are but *our* dreams – provisional, temporary, context-related. But, as part of the activity and mission, in continuity with the dreams of authentic *ecclesia*, our dreams are 'the theatre of the soul' and form part of the activity of soul-making, and of *gathering the fragments.* They are where Psyche and Eros in full mutuality are at play, where we can glimpse the dimension of eternity embodied as Emmanuel among us – although of course not exclusively so.

Even more crucially, dreaming is the eschatological dimension of *ecclesia*. It is entrusted to the pilgrim people to keep the dream alive. Living out of the dream, empowered by God's dream, means giving shape to God's project on earth. As such, this is the most vital dimension of authentic *ecclesia*.

We dare to dream: reconstructing Christian eschatology

When the Cruise missiles were still present at American air bases in England, the Netherlands and Germany, the culture of the Peace Camps which sprang up around them is a powerful memory of a prophetic spirituality of resistance.[11] One of the most transforming memories is of the vigils around the holy days of Easter. Beginning with a shared seder supper on the night of Maundy Thursday, women gathered and were joined by men from Peace groups.[12] (On

Good Friday this would be augmented by people of all ages who simply wanted peace: in fact, the way that longing for peace inspires the coming together of disparate groups is one example of the idea, expressed in the last chapter, of the Church as holding together different forms of communities.) One year at which I was present at Greenham Common, it was fiercely cold – in fact there was a snowstorm. As we read the Passion story of Jesus from the Gospel of Mark – with the soldiers in front of us and the police behind – there was a strong apocalyptic experience. It was as if this story of one man's suffering because of his different vision of how to live had taken on a new and immediate power in our midst. It was not a mere remembering of the past – it was being lived now, as we ourselves reclaimed the dream for which Jesus died. But in the very act of identification I felt there was a sensation of being empowered by the dream: it was as if we were realizing that living out of this dream meant that the dream's power was beginning to blossom in our own context.

The culmination of all human struggles, longings and hopes in the Reign of God is what is usually meant by Christian eschatology. This is the great Christian dream of the end times. Of course, in its traditional meaning of 'the last things', this covers a spectrum of concerns, from the apocalyptic dimension: death, the after-life, judgement, hell and heaven, to related doctrines like purgatory, limbo, prayer for the dead and the tension between individual and collective salvation.[13] Here, my perspective is of the 'last things' as God's dream of justice for the whole of creation, a re-ordering of relations which includes humanity's relations with nature and the environment. Ultimately, even the renewed prophetic imagination for which I have been calling falls short of this reality. As Paul wrote, freely quoting Isaiah 64:4 (although the primary reference is to faith on earth): 'What no eye has seen, nor ear heard, nor the heart of man conceived, what God has prepared for those who love him' (1 Corinthians 2:9). But failure to engage in imagining – and to enact what is imagined and dreamed – is not even to glimpse through a glass darkly. It is to be left with the very Dark Night with which this book is concerned.

It is clear that eschatology is entering a new phase concerning the ancient tension between prophetic and apocalyptic eschatologies. Traditionally, even if the hoped-for state of renewal of the cosmos and second coming was envisaged at the end of time, there were always acts – like hoping, praying and service of neighbour – which were considered as preparation for this. But because of the new developments in understanding the structural causes of injustice, the re-ordering of relations is now worked for on a wider scale. As Monika Hellwig wrote:

What has happened in modern times, partly through the long impact of Christianity and partly through technical, social and political developments in society, is that we have become empowered to act more directly to change the larger structures of our relationships with one another in history. That empowerment has brought with it a *new eschatological exigency*.[14] [My italics]

This new exigency – also seen in the way the approach to the millennium is witnessing an abundance of visionary creativity – is seen in the understanding of the Reign of God as the concrete state of affairs where children do not starve, are not forced into a life of drugs and prostitution in order to stay alive, and where there is an end to conflicts which drive impoverished peoples into fleeing their countries and becoming refugees. Millennial times are times of the Holy Spirit and we are seeing a confluence of the themes of the biblical Jubilee with millenarian thinking[15] – which gives grounds for very real hope, a hope also bursting out of the pages of Pope John Paul's Apostolic Letter *Tertio Millennio Adveniente*.

But there is an eschatological exigency of a different sort. Because of the gravity of the ecological crisis (see Chapter 5), and because of the strong spiritualizing tradition within Christianity, it has become easy to see the crisis as the *end of nature*, the death of nature and the end of time. Eschatology and life after death become viewed as *life after earth*. In a culture where all is disposable and throwaway, nature too is disposable. We can do without all things earthly, because we are only pilgrims here, passing through, so her significance is transient. What is more, our future, the new Jerusalem, is beyond the earth. So, when the earth becomes a spoiled plaything, do not despair, because 'Daddy will give you a new one'.[16] Catherine Keller writes:

> Because the very notion of the end of the world has been distorted by the modern capacity to bring that about – that is, to effect a man-made apocalypse – the meaning of eschatology must also be fundamentally renegotiated. Unless it can meaningfully and effectively address the green apocalypse, Christian theology becomes a trivial pursuit at the end of the second millennium.[17]

The task for authentic *ecclesia*, then, is, first, not a flight from, but a 'reconversion to the earth'.[18] Much ecofeminist theological effort concentrates on what this might mean. For Rosemary Ruether it means that when we die,

> our existence as individuated ego/organism ... dissolves back into the cosmic matrix of matter/energy, from which new centres of individuation arise. It is this matrix, rather than our individuated centres of being, that is 'ever-lasting', that subsists beneath the coming to be and passing away of individuated beings and even planetary worlds.[19]

Dorothee Soelle envisions the restored community in terms of the garden of the book of Genesis, where 'nature, animals and women partake of the joy, the abundance the fullness of the life of the garden'.[20] Sallie McFague, in her vision of the world as the Body of God, sees it also as the cosmic Christ who is the visible, physical presence of God.[21] Elizabeth Green develops this further in terms of the three themes of creation, continuing creation and re-creation, beautifully expressed in terms of Wisdom Christology where the Christ-Sophia is active in creation and history.[22] Just as the earth shook at the dying of the Christ-Sophia, so the earth is involved with the cosmic new birth which is resurrection. This is the very process to which Paul alludes, where 'the whole creation has been groaning in travail until now' (Romans 8:22).

I want to take this process as fundamental for *dreaming ecclesia*, the work, the liturgy of the community which reconstructs eschatology on the basis of a *green apocalypse*. This means discovering and embracing the earth as our ultimate home. Returning to the earth, through the movement of dwelling, I have shown to be the great metanoia of theology.[23] It is here that apocalyptic hope is literally grounded. With every patch of desert which is re-forested and blossoms, every earth-creature saved from extinction, every attempt to live sustainably in the bio-region, the reign of God is glimpsed and earthed. Nor do we need to be one-sidedly physical and material in our re-imagining. As Keller says:

> A gaiocentric eschatology need not bang the spoons of reductionism. Eschatology has been about life after death, and may find new earth-embracing ways of affirming the sustaining and renewing powers of the Spirit and the spirits of life.[24]

This is the crucial point about imagining as *ecclesia*, *ecclesia* which is called to embody the cosmic body of Christ. The old discourse of eschatology is shed like the old wineskins. For the anxiety as to personal survival and well-being gives way to the vision of the communal resurrection story of all earth creatures. This is the redeemed and risen Body. In my book *Redeeming the Dream* I argued that creation and redemption belong together as two sides of the same movement. *Here I argue that creation, redemption and transfiguration of creation belong to what is meant by the cosmic resurrection story*. But that transfiguration is not a metaphysical reality for the end times. Rather, the end times begin now when women, men and children begin to see and hear differently, begin to listen to the cries of wounded creation, begin to act on their vision of healed creation. But they do it as community which refuses the death of nature. They do it as community which is part of nature, and makes space for all earth creatures, community which sees the earth itself as bestower of grace, *green grace*,[25] caught up in the process of transfiguration which is God's dream for the cosmos.

Annie Dillard, in her remarkable book *Pilgrim at Tinker Creek*, describes this process of transfiguration in her intuition that there is a kind of seeing which involves letting-go.[26] Inspired by the girl who was no longer blind and saw the tree 'with lights in it' she set off herself in search of this tree: she did not find it:

> Then one day I was walking along Tinker Creek thinking of nothing at all, and I saw the tree with lights in it. I saw the backyard cedar where the mourning doves roost charged and transfigured, each cell buzzing with flame. I stood on the grass with the lights in it, grass that was wholly fire, utterly focused and utterly dreamed. It was less like seeing, than being for the first time seen, knocked breathless by a powerful glance. The flood of fire abated, but I'm still spending the power . . . The vision comes and goes, mostly goes, but I live for it, for the moment when the mountains open and a new light roars in spate through the crack, and the mountains slam.[27]

This transfiguration experience is what is being offered to us by the Christian doctrine of eschatology. It is an authentic earthed experience, yet at the same time graced, and deeply rooted in the dynamic presence of the Creator God. This is beautifully expressed by the Good Friday Homily of St John Chrysostom:

> The Tree is my eternal salvation. It is my nourishment and my banquet. Amidst its roots I cast my own roots deep; beneath its boughs I grow and expand; as it sighs around me in the breeze I am nourished with delight. Flying from the burning heat, I have pitched my tent in its shadow, and have found a resting place of dewy freshness . . . This is my strait path, my narrow way; this is Jacob's ladder, on which the angels pass up and down, while the Lord in very truth stands at its head. This Tree, vast as heaven itself, rises from earth to the skies, a plant immortal, set firm in the midst between heaven and earth, base of everything that exists, foundation of the universe . . . [28]

The Tree, of course, is the Tree of the Cross — and Christ's suffering is interpreted as yielding cosmic regeneration, in a way which does not separate earth from human healing, nor delay this to a spiritualized, other-worldly universe.

And in the end, a green eschatology is what is truly apocalyptic. It is not grounded in violence, or a failure to face violence by a spiritualizing of the reality of heaven. As Martin Luther said, 'Here I stand', on this ground — but I participate in the reality of heaven when I recognize it as holy. And my hope will be steadfast. As a writer from Chile put it — and these words encapsulate the scriptural longing and believer's conviction that God's dream in Christ will see fulfilment, beginning from this moment:

> I believe that behind the mist the sun waits.
> I believe that beyond the dark night it is raining stars.
> I believe in secret volcanoes and the world below,
> I believe that this lost ship will reach port.
> They will not rob me of hope,
> It shall not be broken,
> It shall not be broken.
>> My voice is filled to overflowing
>> with the desire to sing,
>> the desire to sing.[29]

Notes

1 Toni Morrison, *Beloved* (London: Chatto and Windus/Picador, 1987), pp. 87–8.

2 I have been greatly helped in this task by Grace Jantzen's recent book *Gender, Power and Christian Mysticism* (Cambridge: CUP, 1995).

3 See UNICEF, *I Dream of Peace: Images of War by Children of the Former Jugoslavia* (London: HarperCollins, 1994).

4 For example, Thomas Berry, *The Dream of the Earth* (San Francisco: Sierra Club, 1988); Virginia Fabella and Sun Ai Lee Park (eds), *We Dare to Dream: Doing Theology As Asian Women* (Hong Kong: Asian Women's Resource Centre, 1989); M. Grey, *Redeeming the Dream* (London: SPCK, 1989).

5 Brian Swimme, *The Universe Is a Green Dragon* (Santa Fe: Bear and Co., 1984), p. 47.

6 As I described in Chapter 7.

7 See Jean-Paul Sartre, *L'Imagination* (1936; Paris: Presses Universitaires de France, 1965); Mary Warnock, *Imagination and Time* (London: Faber, 1980); Bernard Lonergan, *Insight* (London: Darton, Longman and Todd, 1983); Sharon Welch, *A Feminist Ethic of Risk* (Minneapolis: Fortress, 1990).

8 Adrian Hastings, *The Shaping of Prophecy* (London: Geoffrey Chapman, 1995), p. 11.

9 Far from refuting the activity of angels, I see their presence and power as far more pervasive and immanent than does orthodox theology. Angels are busy creatures and extraordinarily forgiving of us!

10 I cannot agree with Catherine Keller here who argues that this is a totally anti-ecological new creation if there is no need for the sea. I think the language is extravagant and poetic: if the river of the water of life and the leaves of the trees which are for the healing of the nation (22:3) figure so prominently, there has to be another explanation. Keller actually agrees that it is still possible to read this book ecologically.

11 There is still a presence of women at Greenham Common as well as a Women's Peace Movement which continues to meet at several of the bases.

12 The initiative was led by Pax Christi and Christian CND.

13 For a contemporary summary of the doctrine, and related bibliography, see Monika Hellwig, 'Eschatology' in *Systematic Theology: Roman Catholic Perspectives*, ed. Francis Schüssler

Fiorenza and John P. Galvin (Dublin: Gill and Macmillan, 1992), pp. 673–96. For a feminist reflection, see Catherine Keller, 'Eschatology' in *Dictionary of Feminist Theologies*, ed. Letty Russell and Shannon Clarkson (Louisville, KY: Westminster John Knox, 1996), pp. 86–7.

14 Hellwig, 'Eschatology', p. 685. It has to be confessed that there is not unanimity on this point: 'Cardinal Ratzinger . . . has maintained that the notion of the Reign of God must be kept radically separate from questions of political responsibility for developments in history. He takes issue not only with current developments in systematic theology that include a worldly historical dimension, but he claims that they are based on a false exegesis of the biblical term reign of God . . . for a different, understanding of the relationship between death and the reign of God, see Gisbert Greshake, "Endzeit und Geschichte" in G. Greshake and G. Lohfink (eds), *Naherwartung, Auferstehung, Unsterblichkeit* (Freiburg: Herder, 1975), pp. 11–37': Hellwig, 'Eschatology' p. 684, footnote 12.

15 See, for example, Brian Davies, Mary Grey et al., *The Millennium Jubilee: Theological Reflections Towards the Millennium* (London: CAFOD, 1996).

16 The phrase is Catherine Keller's.

17 Catherine Keller, 'Talking about the weather: the greening of eschatology' in *Ecofeminism and the Sacred*, ed. Carol Adams (New York: Continuum, 1993), p. 36.

18 Rosemary Ruether, cited in Keller, ibid., p. 43.

19 Rosemary Ruether, *Sexism and God-Talk* (London: SCM, 1983), p. 257.

20 D. Soelle, *To Work and To Love: A Theology of Creation* (Philadelphia: Fortress, 1984), pp. 80–1, 150. For an interesting discussion on this theme see Elizabeth Green, 'The travail of creation and the daughters of God: ecofeminism and eschatology', *Ecotheology* 1 (1996), pp. 61–70.

21 Sallie McFague, *The Body of God: An Ecological Theology* (London: SCM, 1993), p. 182.

22 Green, 'The travail of creation', pp. 65–6.

23 The phrase is Keller's, 'Talking about the weather', p. 46.

24 Keller, ibid., p. 47.

25 The phrase is Jay McDaniel's: see *Roots and Wings: Christianity in an Age of Dialogue* (Maryknoll: Orbis, 1995).

26 Annie Dillard, *Pilgrim at Tinker Creek* (New York: Harper and Row, 1974), pp. 33–4.

27 Ibid.

28 St John Chrysostom, Good Friday homily, cited in Bishop Kallistos, 'From creation to the Creator', *Ecotheology* 2 (January 1997).

29 From Hans-Georg Link (ed.), *Confessing Our Faith Around the World*, vol. 4: *South America* (Geneva: WCC, 1985); cited from *A CAFOD Prayerbook*, compiled by Jane King (London: CAFOD, 1995), p. 3.

PART THREE

THE SHAPING OF THE DREAM AND THE RECOVERY OF SOUL

We do not want less religion, we want more; but it must be a religion that gets its orientation from the Kingdom of God. To concentrate our efforts on personal salvation, as orthodoxy has done, or on soul culture, as liberalism has done, comes close to refined selfishness. All of us who have been trained in egotistic religion need a conversion to Christian Christianity, even if we are Bishops or theological professors. Seek ye first the Kingdom of God, and God's righteousness, and the salvation of your souls will be added to you.

(Walter Rauschenbusch, *Christianizing the Social Order* (New York: Macmillan, 1919), pp. 464–5)

9

BREAKING THE DEADLOCK: NEW MODELS OF AUTHORITY, POWER AND LEADERSHIP

> I believe in change: change personal, and change in society. I have experienced
> a revolution (unfinished, without question, but one whose order is everywhere
> on view) in the South. And I grew up – until I refused to go – in the Methodist
> church, which taught me that Paul will sometimes change on the way to
> Damascus, and that Moses – that beloved old man – went through so many
> changes he made God mad.
>
> (Alice Walker[1])

> We will reflect together on the needs and challenges facing us. We will evaluate
> the resources we have and how best to use them . . . We will do our best to work
> collaboratively with each other, so that the result is a real 'conspiratio' – a
> breathing together of the breath of the Holy Spirit who inspires all our work and
> leads us ever more deeply into the truths of the Gospel.
>
> (Bishop Crispian Hollis[2])

Journeying, dwelling, traditioning, transforming and dreaming – I have
explored all these as dimensions of Church within the context of the shaking of
the foundations and the collective loss of soul in Western society. But if these
five movements are to change anything, it will be against the background of the
tensions and dissensions which now cause so much anguish. The challenge is to
develop a new approach in order to break the seeming deadlock, the impasse
and deeply rooted tensions between the two principal ways of being Church
now operational, the prophetic and the institutional. For it is exactly in the areas
of concepts of authority, of the way power is exercised and the styles of
leadership engendered by the different notions of *ecclesia* that these tensions are
rife. *It is here that the darkest hour of the long Dark Night is experienced.*

This chapter begins to trace a way out of deadlock. The first feature which
has emerged from the five strands explored in Part Two is that from the
resources of Christianity[3] come possibilities for the transformation of society –
the principal task of authentic community (see Chapter 7). Secondly, despite the

critical stance taken, the prophetic groups whose views are expressed here –
who adopt the stance of creative boundary living – do so out of a tremendous
love for the Church. Elisabeth Fiorenza has frequently said of women that 'we
are not quitters'. Women love the Church and do not want to leave. Like the
policemen in Gilbert and Sullivan's much-loved comic opera *Pirates of Pen-
zance*, who never quite summon the courage to go to battle, we deserve the
taunt 'Yes but you don't go!'

Not that there should be any minimalizing of the suffering and the damage
inflicted on both the Church's integrity and the individuals concerned, when,
for example, someone of the stature of Bishop Jacques Gaillot is demoted from
his episcopal ministry; when five feminist theologians, appointed to professorial
chairs in universities in Germany and Switzerland, are blocked from their
appointments by the Vatican;[4] when the liberation theologian from Sri Lanka,
Tissa Balasuriya, has to swear a long and detailed oath of allegiance to every
aspect of the teaching of the magisterium to prove his loyalty and status as
Catholic theologian; and when the rector of a seminary in El Salvador orders all
books and articles written by liberation theologians to be removed from the
seminary library.[5] (And these are only small examples of a far longer catalogue
of woes.) To look at the issue of authority from the other side of the coin, the
uproar caused by the case of the Scottish bishop, Roderick Wright, who
recently disappeared with one woman, was revealed to have had a long-
standing affair with another, by whom he had a fifteen-year-old son, and who
then sold his story to the tabloids, has raised problems of a different kind.[6]
Clearly it raises the status of the authority of celibacy; it raises also the question
of the justice of the way women have been treated by priests and Church
officials who carry on clandestine affairs;[7] but it also raises the issue of the
integrity of witness of Church leaders themselves.

But alongside this needs to be set the witness of a new and very positive
current of thinking. As the quotation from Bishop Crispian Hollis's speech at
the beginning of this chapter shows, in the Roman Catholic Church there is
now a very genuine commitment to collaborative ministry[8] between laity and
clergy. Indeed, the Bishop speaks of 'the seeds of a revolution in the way in
which we live and work in the Church today'.[9] The National Board of Catholic
Women has achieved channels of communication with the Bishops' Conference
on such crucial topics as violence against women.[10] Bishop Hollis in his own
diocese has himself taken a very active and critical stance on the issue of clergy
abuse of children and child abuse in general. There are also initiatives taken –
for example by Bishop David Konstant – towards ministry and solidarity with
gay communities. However timid and inchoate these initiatives may seem,

however inadequate in the face of the scale of the problem, one can still speak of a growing recognition among the hierarchy of the Roman Catholic Church of the seriousness of many of these issues: it was striking that on his appointment as President of Ushaw College, Fr Jim O'Keefe spoke of the deficiency in education on sexuality and masculinity among seminarians. 'Male-dominated structures – including churches – are a denial of the Trinity', he said.[11]

It would be easy to dismiss these examples as being too few and too late, or as a superficial response to a far more deep-seated problem. After all, the inflexibility with regard to women's ordination and position of women in decision-making structures is largely unchanged. But I am convinced that there is an energy and a commitment to change, and a belief that the Church – seen now as the whole pilgrim people of God – has the humility and ability for a conversion which is more far-reaching. As I said earlier, the groundswell of prophetic groups, deeply loyal to the ideals of *authentic ecclesia*, is increasing – and it is from *authentic ecclesia* as the discipleship community seeking truth and justices that the Church must seek to fashion its identity.

To put flesh on the bones of a new understanding, through re-weaving the strands of journeying, dwelling, traditioning, transforming and dreaming in our specific context, the next task is to re-imagine the current models of authority, power and leadership; where these are based on the paradigm of domination and dominion, re-imaging them on the basis of community, communion and transformed relationships of justice is the goal. I first look at the current models of leadership, challenging them specifically from the experience of women and excluded groups, asking on what basis they function and then rooting an alternative re-imagining of power and authority in the faithful re-creation of the praxis and ministry of Jesus and the first disciples. This is a *journeying* which includes all women, men and children, specifically seeking to begin with the contribution of excluded groups; it is *dwelling* – in the places of the forsaken, in the consciousness of the acute suffering of our original *economy, oikos*, the planet;[12] it is *traditioning*, in placing ourselves in continuity with the moment and movements from Christian past and present which nurture and sustain our vision; it is *transforming*, since, in recognizing changed notions of authority and leadership, people are enabled to act on their deepest intuitions, and begin to play a role in an institution in which up till now they have been relegated to the sidelines, or to passive obedience. And in nourishing our dreams of a renewed authority, *dreaming ecclesia* makes embodiments of the Reign of God not remote possibilities but tangible joy.

Patterns of leadership

Letty Russell has written that in our patriarchal society, power and authority are usually associated with domination, competition and control:

> ... do they need to be understood this way? From the perspective of Christian gospel and from the perspective of feminist theory the answer is *no*. Power and authority can be exercised through domination, and they most frequently are, in a world patterned by patriarchal paradigms of reality. But they can also be exercised through empowerment and authorizing, as they sometimes are where people are seeking to live out the gospel vision of shared community of service.[13]

But women in leadership positions have few role models to inspire the leadership for transformation of which I speak. Despite the fact that all great spiritual leaders, for example, Jesus, Buddha, Gandhi, Muhammad, have offered their followers a way – which they themselves have embodied – this has not necessarily been helpful to women. Centuries of exclusion from leadership roles has taken a painful toll – and centuries of being at the receiving end of authority as domination and control has increased this. Feminist scholars are all too painfully aware of how women have to struggle so desperately to attain their positions, that being *co-opted into existing models* in order to be approved of is the only option for survival. This is exactly the point of tension for women who have been recently ordained in the Church of England. Can a woman be a leader in the Church without being sucked into destructive patterns of patriarchal behaviour? It is almost the same as asking whether a woman can be a company director without being drawn into patterns of decision-making which privilege the rich and maintain an ethics based on profit-making for the few, regardless of the global impact on many poor communities.

Here I try to identify building blocks or tools emerging from the insights of feminist liberation theology, specifically for women as leaders for change, but also as catalysts for transformation in Church and society.[14] The pre-requisite for authentic ecclesial leadership is of course to be steeped in *practical wisdom – sophia wisdom* – a wisdom which connects being, doing, making and knowing with a deep compassion. The ancient biblical tradition insisting on the wisdom of the ruler carries its own authority. This is a *passionate wisdom* which sees beyond the dualisms – the vicious racist, sexist and heterosexist dualisms which continue to underpin poverty and discrimination and legitimize the domination of one sex by another. Secondly, from this wisdom springs a set of skills rooted in a *vision* of transformed society. Without being steeped in the vision – as the last chapter has argued – our ideas of empowerment and change are built on shifting sands and fantasy. What gives great hope is that the prophetic groups I have been describing, following the message of the parable of the woman with the measure of yeast who leavens the whole bread (Luke 13:20), are engaging constructively with society: they do not simply remain on the margins, incurring the risk of being completely ignored and trivialized. Empowerment from *sophia wisdom* is not an arbitrary quality, but based on the scriptural fact that authority is rooted in Christ and ultimately in God, source of all wisdom: millennial times could be the moment when not only leaders, but the communities to which they are accountable, recognize that it is not power, money or qualifications which are crucial, but wisdom – practical, compassionate, drawing its treasures from past and present.

Thirdly, a theology for change and empowerment must be one of *resistance* and at the same time one of *persistence*. Think of the Gospel story of the judge who gave way to the insistent pleas of the widow. He basically caved in because she went on and on . . . (Luke 18:1–7). She bothered him. I think that exactly the same courage is needed – the courage to be, to go on and on despite the opposition (but at times to be a bit more subtle!). Fourthly, *prophetic witness* also plays a vital part in leadership for change. It is first and foremost a witness to Christ as prophet, and his handing on of this mission to the whole Church. So it is a witness and fidelity to authentic *ecclesia* as prophet: and *ecclesia* as *discipleship of equals*[15] calls on *both* her daughters and her sons to exercise this role. The prophetic integrity of *ecclesia* depends on the call to prioritize the situation of the poorest of the poor, as intense a call today as it was in New Testament times. Prophetic integrity is contextualized, for example, in the power of non-violent pacifism: the impact of both the dramatic symbolic action as well as the life-style, in solidarity with more conventional Peace groups, on a society so addicted to weapons and the arms trade cannot be over-estimated. Dorothy Day in the United States, Petra Kelly in Germany, both made the connections between non-violent living, eco-justice and poverty, and took stances of prophetic witness which are still, after their deaths, powerful today.[16] But the authority of this is derived from its congruence with prophetic action in the Hebrew Scriptures and because of the authority of the non-violent style of living in Jesus' vision of the Kingdom.

In Chapter 6, 'Traditioning', I suggested the image of Miriam's Well, to inspire a creative remembering of resources. Miriam is also a figure who embodies the skills of prophetic witness, and inspires a new style of leadership. 'It all began with Miriam' is the title of Catharina Halkes' book, referred to earlier.[17] It began with Miriam in at least three senses: she is the first woman leader from the biblical tradition. She is also a leader in times of great suffering and oppression. Miriam knew what it was to be poor, to be a refugee, to be without water in the desert. But, thirdly, she is also the first woman leader from our tradition to be forgotten! It is Moses who is honoured as the great prophet and leader, and Miriam who is forgotten, until – within the Christian tradition at least – the new Miriam, Mary, became the mother of Jesus. Or until a group of Jewish women began to create their own Passover, which they called Miriam's Telling.[18] Yet, as Carol Ochs tells us, in her inspiring article 'Miriam's Way', referred to earlier (p. 51),

> Miriam's Way gives us tools for thinking about everything from the Mosaic account of Creation, through the pain between generations that fills the Torah, to the wonder of raising children who surpass us ... After years of wandering in the desert, building worlds of meaning and value, and encountering Nothing, we finally recognize the essential truth of that Way: our lives are precious gifts in which we can find the Divine presence.[19]

Remembering Miriam is thus remembering prophetic leadership. Miriam led her sisters in the dance, a kind of leadership which calls forth a community to embody its hopes and its stories in music, song, poetry and movement. Elisabeth Moltmann-Wendel suggests that Miriam's Way connects with an older culture, perhaps even a pre-patriarchal culture which respected women's gifts of prophetic story-telling and music.[20]

Miriam and the many women who have gone before as leaders have been not just un-remembered, *but dismembered*. So Miriam is now reclaimed as a leader who cared for innocent life: in the way she saved the baby Moses, and her possible association with the community of women midwives who, under the oppression of Pharaoh, were saving the baby boys of the children of Israel from being killed (Exodus 1:15–21). Miriam is reclaimed now as counselling and consoling the women when Moses was receiving the revelation on Mount Sinai. Miriam was present as strength, when – just as women struggled to keep community alive during the recent war in Bosnia – husbands and sons were killed in battle, when their babies and little children died through starving or through sickness and the many hardships of being pilgrims in the desert; Miriam led them in songs of lament for their dead loved ones and kept alive the spark of hope in them as the vision of the Promised Land faded from their imaginations – although it never entirely faded.

The rhetoric makes it seem so easy: the Bible tells the story of the giant Goliath being defeated by little David. Another story tells of a little sparrow on its back in the road, its feeble legs flailing desperately in the air. A horseman comes riding by, reins his horse and asks sarcastically 'What do you think you are doing?' 'Well', said the sparrow, 'I heard that the sky will fall in today and I am trying to hold it up.' The horseman then said mockingly 'And do you really think that you, feeble creature that you are, can make any difference to the scale of the disaster?' 'Well', said the sparrow, 'one does what one can.'[21] The power of the powerless, drawn on by all the liberation theologies, the little people, the Davids, the clowns and the fools, if we could really seize it, would it bring down the giants of today, the World Bank, the IMF, the 'Structural Adjustment' programmes, the multi-nationals, the corporations, the drug barons, the media moguls? Is there any effective power, any effective basis for authority with which to offer an alternative to the 'power and might' of control and domination? And if ordinary women and men in the churches do have this power and authority by virtue of the mission of baptism and the commitment of the baptismal community, what prevents us claiming its transforming potential? Is it not at least possible that we have allowed ourselves to live alienated from the power which could change us and our culture from the 'lies, secrets and silence' which buy into the violence which makes women's lives and the lives of many marginalized groups full of fear and misery?

Too many diseased forms of leadership and power-relations prolong this alienation. Secular power is too often experienced in patters of leadership not only hierarchical but *kyriarchal*.[22] Yet it is a naïve over-simplification to state that women are powerless victims of men as oppressors, an over-simplification which prolongs dualism and ignores the complexities of the ways in which women and men participate in configurations of power. Power as dominance, as military aggression, for example, affects the lives of the vulnerable – children, women and men – on a global scale. One million children starve in Iraq in the wake of the Allied invasion in the Gulf War. In 1996, in the wake of renewed American bombings, the cycle of fleeing refugees, disease and poverty is, tragically, beginning again. It is easy to see the power of dominance when lived out in patterns of leadership like dictatorships and tyrannies, and as legitimated power in war, torture and in some fascist groups. There it is undisguised and undeniably ugly. But it is less easy to see it in, for example, the effects of 'Structural Adjustment' programmes, and unjust land systems, where, in many parts of the world, a few rich landowners control vast estates, poor people being forced to sell themselves and their children as bonded labourers (modern 'slaves'). Here, many forms of the power of domination come together to keep the lives of women, men and children in abject poverty. This pattern of leadership which sees power as domination, the ideology which keeps the killing systems of domination/submission alive, also considers that compassion is the emotion of the weak. For example, to be black, a woman or a girl child, a lower-caste woman in India, is to suffer a triple oppression, legitimized by the legal system. But if that woman is in Europe, she is just as vulnerable to the many faces of poverty – and the law has no more compassion in cases of asylum and deportations.

Nor is the leadership of the *guru* more effective in dismantling the 'powers' which hold society in such a vicious grip. The kind of authority wielded by the guru is not the authority of domination but a more charismatic type. The respect and reverence which a person like Gandhi evoked was able to influence people to follow his non-violent life-style of peace and love of village life. But Hitler himself had enormous charismatic authority. Charisma coupled with a mythology which reached people at a psychic level, and ready access to military might, meant that power became almost demonic in character. Charismatic power which focuses on the personality of the guru – be that guru male or female – is ultimately crippling for the followers who become dependent, alienated from their own sources of energy. The *authentic* leader figure puts disciples in touch with their own source of power, strength and authority. 'Touching our strength' (the words are of the poet Adrienne Rich) means being energized by the roots of our own power. Then we know ourselves called out of isolation, alienation and separation. Yet our isolation was no accident, but structurally organized and maintained.[23] This is society's most effective trick: to isolate us from each other through poverty, unemployment, shame; then the power of solidarity is lost. We become sisters and brothers in solidarity, *compañeras*, when we discover each other, moved by *power-in-relation*, which is the point at which we touch the divine roots of our being.[24] And this is the authentic source of power, to know oneself as God's good creation, affirmed and loved.

To be able to touch this power which imagines a new creation and acts as midwife to its birth as *ecclesial*, as *sparked off by community praxis*, could be the very catalyst to lead us out of the Dark Night. First, I explore how this was the power and authority which animated Christ and the first Christian communities who tried to embody his vision.

Jesus and the model of mutual empowerment

It can appear to be the most nostalgic of naïveties to return to the praxis and life-style of Jesus of Nazareth to ground a new understanding of power. In one sense the Christian Church can never turn the clock back and ignore the troubled, muddled history of authority in the Church, the ever-present tension between charism and office and the urgency of the need for good governance in this, the time of fragmented foundations of society. Time and again the breakaway sects which try to reproduce the simplicity and what they judge to be the anti-world stance of the Gospels become shipwrecked on the need for continuity, order and authority. Millenarianism is once more in the air, with its doom and gloom apocalyptical discourse: it is once again time to go to the mountains to await the second coming. Thus the repudiation of all that is worldly, and with it the doctrinal and sacramental superstructures, which, it can be argued, should be jettisoned in the urgency of the end times.

On the one hand, it is always time to go to the Holy Mountain, with a stance of waiting and expectation.[25] But it is vital to do this, not in a world-fleeing sense, but in a deeper engagement with the 'powers' which threaten destruction.[26] It is with full recognition of the need for good government, of the need to balance the authority of local community with universal *ecclesia*, of the need for the See of Rome to recognize the authority of Constantinople, Canterbury and Moscow, that this exploration of the basis of Jesus' authority is made.

Immediately the paradox must be grappled: how can a man whose mission appeared to be a spectacular failure be a role model for power and authority? Yet the first striking aspect of Jesus of Nazareth seems that he spoke with authority, an authority which had an almost spell-binding effect on those who listened to him.[27] Nor should this authority be trivialized by understanding Jesus merely as faith-healer and miracle-worker. He was both of these. No doubt an element of his following sought signs, wonders and an excitement which relieved the desperation of poverty. But Jesus was first and foremost an authoritative *teacher*, even if it is impossible to distinguish what he said, what he did, who he was and the community life-style in which all of this was manifested. This is why the configurations of relational power lived and embodied by Jesus needs to be reclaimed.

For Jesus, as Rosemary Ruether has pointed out, is the *kenosis of patriarchy*. In contrast with the patriarchal patterns of hierarchical domination, the life-style of messianic community – and of those communities which remain faithful to this witness – is one of mutual empowerment.[28] It is embodied in the table-fellowship, the model of hospitality where Jesus ate with women of the streets, with sinners, with tax collectors; where he broke taboos against speaking with a haemorrhaging woman, an adulterous woman, a foreign woman, with lepers, with children. It is embodied in the way his teaching insisted that 'I do not call you servants ... but friends' (John 15:15) with the insistence that hierarchical rank was not what relationships in the Kingdom were about (Mark 9:33–37); rather, that it was precisely by fidelity to the Kingdom vision that people – including women – were to be valued.[29]

Jesus proclaimed the *kenosis* of patriarchy because the God with whom he was in intimate communion was revealed as a *kenotic Godhead*. All power comes from this God:

> 'Do you not know that I have power to release you, and power to crucify you?' [asked Pontius Pilate]. Jesus answered him, 'You would have no power over me unless it had been given you from above'. (John 19:10–11)

Pilate's authority (*exousia* is the Greek word), the authority of office, and in this case the military authority of a colonizing force, had no real power over Jesus unless God was allowing this. God's *authentic exousia* is in contrast with Pilate's *oppressive exousia*. But God's power is revealed in vulnerability: power-in-vulnerability, because this man, tortured, flogged, abandoned by his friends, and in the extremes of humiliation, by keeping alive the vision of the just relating of the kin-dom, the power of just relating, showed the powers of kyriarchy as empty, as having no authenticity. Jesus was vulnerable because God's power is manifest in vulnerability. But even in this abandonment, the healing strength of relational power, the openness to relation, could not be quenched. 'Weep not for me, but for yourselves and for your children', cried Jesus to the daughters of Jerusalem (Luke 23:28). The power of compassion was still being poured out. The power of forgiveness was freely given from the cross itself. But if relational power needs an element of mutuality, that too was present in that Jesus was supported by the women who followed him from Galilee. He, the Teacher, from the beginning of his ministry is revealed as being open not only to the vulnerability, but to the insights, the relational strengths of others in the Messianic community.

This is absolutely basic to understanding the humanity of Jesus. As Rita Brock has written:

> At the earliest part of our lives we are dependent on the loving power of others to nurture us. Their failure to do so has serious consequences. We are broken by the world of our relationships before we are able to defend ourselves.[30]

That Jesus received 'grace', 'heart', 'original grace' in the form of nurture from his mother, and from the Jewish community which nurtured him, became the source of his authority, the empowerment of giving and receiving in relationship and community. The element of mutuality is remarkable in the way Jesus was able to listen, learn and act, in the healing stories, for example, of the Samaritan woman at the well (John 4), the story of the Syro-Phoenician woman (Mark 7:24–30) and that of the Roman centurion (Luke 7:1–10). But the often missed, crucial point for today is that the messianic community was a community of *poor people*, desperate, often hungry, eking out a living on the margins of a society where Romans lived in luxury. Yet these were the people who, after the Easter/Pentecost event, spoke, acted and healed with authority out of their newborn sense of being empowered, and who, women and men, within a few years began travelling far beyond the fishing villages of Galilee, to live out the message of healing power, and the proclamation of the authoritative word, in ever new contexts.

In a contemporary context we seek again the *kenosis* of patriarchy through the rediscovery and the re-privileging of the authority of poor communities. This does not mean the idealizing of poverty. As Reb Tevye in *Fiddler on the Roof* exclaimed, 'It's no great thing to be poor!' Nor does it mean substituting the (lost) idea of *sensus fidelium* (agreement of the faithful) for hierarchical authority.[31] Just as the priorities of the kin-dom of right relations sprang from the material realities of poor people – this being where Christ's language of power originates – so giving back to poor communities the authority of their own voice, and not speaking or acting for them, is recovering the reality of mutual empowerment. But poor communities have identity and context. The Christian Church has so over-identified itself with Eurocentric structures and mindset that it has ideologized Christ's language of poverty and suffering, while at the same time robbing poor people who are actually living out lives of generosity, compassion and power-in-weakness, of the authority of witnessing to the Kingdom.

Without the input of the understandings of power, authority and leadership from the underside of history, Church and society can never move on from the flawed understandings which inhibit authentic fidelity to the Gospel and thus the task of transformation of society. I seek now some practical ways forward.

Moving forward ...

With the wisdom of Sophia and trusting this vision of mutual empowerment, rooted in the kin-dom of right relations, the next step is to take the power of naming into our hands: by discerning what the Church loses by failing to empower women, the non-ordained, the many marginalized groups, the hope is to explore whether a new phoenix can arise, new forms of power and authority from the ashes of exclusion to move us beyond the Dark Night.

First, there is growing power in solidarity and in networking. The power which brings out of isolation and opens up new possibilities with genuine promise of healing is living again the authentic scriptural vision. Second, women, laypeople and many minority groups are empowered by listening, hearing, discerning each other's wisdom, by acknowledging the truth of each other, by creating 'safe spaces', like a clearing in the forest, where stories can be told. The words of the Greek tragedy *Medea* can ring once again:

> Flow backwards to your sources, sacred rivers . . .
> And let the world's great order be reversed . . .
> Stories shall now turn my condition to a fair one,
> Women shall now be paid their due.[32]

The wonderful character from the black American woman novelist Toni Morrison in her novel *Beloved*, namely, Baby Suggs, holy, cited at the beginning of Chapter 8, in the midst of slavery in the deep South lived out a strikingly empowering model of authority. She empowered her people *with her great big heart*, showing them the power of seeing things differently. In other words, she recovered for them the power of the community's vision and memory.

Just as it was with the earthly Jesus, there is power in our compassion, in our empathy, in our sensitivity. If we have the heart of Baby Suggs, holy, we meet each other at the point of pain, and we stay there. There is a lot of mystification in talk about the Dark Night of the soul. *The Dark Night of the body is just as painful.* But when body and spirit are crushed – that is a real dark night of lostness, pain and confusion. But in that time when all solutions have failed, compassion and the 'boundless heart' are the sources of strength.

It is also crucial to be in touch with the power and authority of a new symbolic system: in our redeeming communities women and men together need to become myth-makers, storytellers of a new symbolic order. Whereas women have suffered enough from the symbolism of being fallen Eve, fallen angels, or the reverse symbolism of being 'angel in the house', men have not been helped towards discovering more just configurations of the meaning of masculinity. Women are neither angels nor monsters – but creatures of flesh and blood, both fierce and tender. It is damaging for both men and women to continue to operate with idealizing or demonizing stereotypes of women. Because women are banned from the altar (in the Roman Catholic Church at least), it is even more vital to tell the stories of the sacred power of women; but to tell the tales in such a way that women are generous and make room in these new creative modes of authority we are creating for just partnerships with men, just partnerships within a re-imaged pattern of ordained priesthood. Hospitality – to each other, to the earth and to God – can become again the pattern of redeemed community.[33]

Women also take strength from the authority and power they have had to sustain community and culture. Although a better analysis is needed as to how, in many societies, women have been co-opted and collude in passing on damaging cultural norms, yet at the same time the strength of women in war and crisis is often the yeast which binds community. Marvelling at the high percentage of women in Parliament in Sweden and Norway, compared with Britain (9 per cent) and France (7 per cent), I am told that this is not due to feminism, but to a much older tradition. In Norway, when the men were away fishing for many months of the year, it was the women who held society together, who were the leaders in fact. So has it always been when men went to war and to hunt: but the problem has been that the stories of conquest make the history books, not the stories of community-creating and sustaining.

Healthy models of authority are built on the power of good communication. In theory women are good at this: statistically at the moment girls are doing better at school than boys. Girls like reading and communicating. In fact it is a serious educational problem for boys today – in Western culture at least – that it is frequently unacceptable to their peer group to be occupied like this. But women's communication is frequently downgraded as gossip, chatter, trivial talk. So if women and men really do have 'the dream of a common language'[34] or 'a common language for the dream', this power has to be seized, in order to facilitate communication. Initially I am speaking of empowering grassroots groups to articulate, and those in power to listen. But actually we are working to build a new model of authority where the voices of the marginalized are recognized as having the authority of living out the witness of the humiliated Christ in the world.

Next, we need to develop our skills in learning different kinds of languages: I do not mean, useful though this is, speaking many 'foreign' languages. But language is power and power structures are reflected in language. Yet to speak inclusively, avoiding dualisms, is often seen as lacking in incisiveness. But it is rare to find Church authorities who have a deep understanding as to what it has meant to women not to have been addressed *specifically* in worship all these years. This is the challenge: how can Christians talk *effectively* and *with authority* to politicians, to economists and managers of the World Bank? The peace processes are in such trouble at the moment. Surely it is those who have so much *hidden* experience and memory of sustaining community and reconciling differences who can develop skills of mediation, facilitating people being able to hear each other? Women's networks – as well as many Justice and Peace Groups – have begun to develop skills of hearing each other's diversity, of respecting each other's differences, even to admitting that the power of white women has colluded in the oppression of black women and that the privileged position of heterosexual women has shared in marginalizing lesbian women. But in the context of ecclesial authority these skills could become languages of mediation, building bridges across the chasms of incomprehension and mutual mistrust.

Thus the power offered as transforming power is not the power of dominance, manipulative power or charismatic power: it is a power which is shared, relational, inclusive, the life-giving power of mutuality. This is what is truly Christic, truly of the holy *Ruah* of the vulnerable God, who refuses the artificial boundaries of office and status. Relational power is based on speaking words of truth – the truth of the dignity of humanity and all earth creatures, the truth of the earth being our common home. The truth of the *commonwealth*, or the wealth we hold in common, the connections in which we live, move and have our being.

But how could we live from this relational power when society – and too often, the Church – operates from the model of control and domination? In other words, how should we live to move beyond the Dark Night? What kind of spirituality will move us out of the impasse?

Notes

1 Alice Walker, *In Search of Our Mothers' Gardens* (New York: Harcourt Brace Jovanovich, 1983), p. 17.
2 Bishop Crispian Hollis, Opening Address, Joint Council of Priests and Laity, Park Place, Wickham, Hants, 20/21 October 1995.
3 There are of course resources in all the great faiths, but this book focuses on Christian ecclesiology.
4 At the moment of writing – October 1996 – three have now been successfully installed.
5 See Fr John Medcalf, 'Trouble in the seminary' in Letters to the Editor, *The Tablet* (31 August 1996).
6 See the reports in *The Guardian, The Times, The Daily Telegraph*, Saturday, 21 September 1996. The *Tablet* editorial was written before the news of the long-standing affair broke: it was therefore treated as an occasion to re-visit the celibacy issue.
7 See Marie Fortune, *Is Nothing Sacred? When Sex Invades the Pastoral Relationship* (San Francisco: Harper and Row, 1989).
8 For the official Report from the Working Party on Collaborative Ministry of the Roman Catholic bishops of England and Wales, see *The Sign We Give* (Chelmsford: Matthew James, on behalf of the Bishops' Conference, 1995).
9 Ibid., p. 7.
10 See Report by the National Board of Catholic Women on Domestic Violence,
11 See *The Tablet* (13 July 1996): 'Ushaw's new President challenges sinful masculinity', p. 937.

12 The root meaning of 'economy', *oikonomia* or 'the rule of our common household', recalls us to a level profounder than the merely monetary. It suggests a balance, or ordering, inclusive of all living things within this fragile web of life. Thus *oikos*, 'home', *oikia*, 'household', do not primarily refer to a building, or even a social network, but to the shaping of our communal lives.

13 Letty Russell, *Household of Freedom: Authority in Feminist Theology* (Philadelphia: Westminster, 1987), p. 23.

14 Some of the material for this chapter is a re-working of my keynote speech at the Women's Synod in Gmünden, Austria, July 1996, 'Empowered to lead: Sophia's daughters blaze a trail'.

15 The phrase is Elisabeth Schüssler Fiorenza's: *In Memory of Her* (London: SCM, 1980).

16 For Petra Kelly, see Sara Parkin, *The Life and Death of Petra Kelly* (London: HarperCollins Pandora, 1994); for Dorothy Day, see her autobiography *The Long Loneliness* (San Francisco: Harper & Row, 1981).

17 Catharina Halkes, *Met Miriam is alles Begonnen* (Baarn: Ten Have, 1980).

18 See Eleanor Broner, *The Telling* (HarperSanFrancisco, 1993).

19 Carol Ochs, 'Miriam's Way', *Crosscurrents* (Winter 1995), pp. 493–509, quotation from p. 509.

20 Elisabeth Moltmann-Wendel, Heidemarie Langer and Herta Leistner, *Met Miriam door de Rietzee* (Stuttgart, 1983; Boxtel, 1985).

21 Original source unknown. I paraphrased this from Joan Chittister, *Winds of Change: Women Challenge the Church* (London: Sheed and Ward, 1986), p. 15.

22 This is Elisabeth Schüssler Fiorenza's word for the lordship of dominance and submission, which justifies one race (white), dominating over another (black), the dominance of one sex over another and the dominance of the northern hemisphere which increases its prosperity while the South starves.

23 See the analysis of sin as separation in *The Wisdom of Fools?* (London: SCM, 1993), pp. 67ff., 117–18; also Catherine Keller, *From a Broken Web* (Boston: Beacon, 1986).

24 *Power-in-relation* is the expression of Carter Heyward in *The Redemption of God: A Theology of Mutual Relation* (Washington, DC: University of America Press, 1980), ch. 1, 'In the beginning is the relation', pp. 1–21. But the entire book is a working out of this central idea.

25 This, a dimension of spirituality, will be discussed in Chapter 10.

26 See Walter Wink, *Engaging the Powers: Discernment and Resistance in a World of Domination* (Minneapolis: Fortress, 1992).

27 For example, Mark 1:22: 'And they were astonished at his teaching, for he taught them as one who had authority, and not as the scribes'; 1:27: 'What is this? A new teaching! With authority he commands even the unclean spirits and they obey him.'

28 See Rosemary Radford Ruether, *Sexism and God-Talk* (London: SCM, 1983); Heyward, *The Redemption of God*; Rita Nakashima Brock, *Journeys by Heart: A Christology of Erotic Power* (New York: Crossroad, 1988).

29 For instance, Luke 8:21: 'My mother and my brethren are those who hear the word of God and do it'; Luke 11:28: '"Blessed is the womb that bore you and the breasts that you sucked!" But he said, "Blessed rather are those who hear the word of God and keep it!"'

30 Brock, *Journeys by Heart*, p. 16.

31 This is not to underestimate the need to recover the *sensus fidelium*. But I am convinced that

if we could re-configure our notions of power and authority on the basis of listening to the excluded groups, the way would be opened up for re-valuing the *sensus fidelium*.

32 Euripides, *Medea*, tr. Rex Warner (University of Chicago Press, 1970), lines 410–20.

33 Hospitality as a dimension of Church is a priority for Letty Russell, *Church in the Round* (Louisville, KY: Westminster John Knox, 1993), and was discussed in the previous chapter.

34 The title of Adrienne Rich's book of poems, *The Dream of a Common Language* (New York: W. & W. Norton, 1978).

A SPIRITUALITY FOR THE DARK NIGHT

Dear sisters and brothers, with the energy of the Holy Spirit let us tear apart all walls of division and the culture of death that separates us. And let us participate in the Holy Spirit's economy of life, fighting for our life on this earth in solidarity with all living beings and building communities for justice, peace and the integrity of creation. Wild wind of the Holy Spirit, blow to us. Let us welcome her, letting ourselves go in her wild rhythm of life. Come, Holy Spirit, renew the whole creation. Amen!

(Chung Hyun Kyung[1])

At times, maintaining a Catholic spirituality feels like a matter of survival. Living with oppressive church structures and male-centered theology is torture, but *rejecting Catholic spiritual riches is starvation.*

(Joann Wolski Conn[2]).

These quotations express something of the ambiguity of the area of spirituality. Is the weight of tradition to be experienced as burden, or can its spiritual resources enable us to glimpse the light at the end of the Dark Night? This chapter seeks a spirituality to sustain and enable the process. Here spirituality is understood as a tool, as a set of practices and disciplines which embody in ordinary living the five dimensions of *ecclesia* which have been explored – journeying, dwelling, traditioning, transforming and dreaming.

But the first hurdle to be overcome is the meaning of spirituality itself. It is a baffling experience to survey the number of spiritualities on offer today and to sample their diversity: from charismatic to political, from Ignatian to Benedictine, from the prayer of silence to evangelical hymn-singing, from indigenous Indian to mainstream Christian sacramental, from the desert experience to aromatherapy, a groaning smorgasbord is set with ever-new brands of 'spiritual experience'. What kind of criteria will determine the kind of spirituality to bring us out of the Dark Night?

Sheer diversity is not the only problem. The need to discern which kind of spirituality has been hi-jacked by the spirit of the age is urgent. The fact that the word itself is not so ancient casts suspicion on certain currents of spirituality.[3] Not everything which goes by the name of spirituality bears any resemblance to what this might mean as a charism of Church. In an age of fragmentation (see Chapter 1), where competitive individualism reigns, there is an uneasy marriage between the self-indulgence of the 'me-generation' and a kind of 'salvation-in-the-sauna' mentality. By saying this in no way do I want to undervalue the enormous good which attention to bodily needs and physical exercise is achieving. A priority of feminist theology – and all liberation theologies – is to insist on paying attention to bodiliness and the quality of the material context in which ordinary people – especially poor people, and most especially poor women – live out their spiritual quest. The anxiety stems from the accent placed on using an *excess* of self-indulgent practices to relieve stress and enable 'the good life', now being culturally interpreted as the acquisition and consumption of material goods, eating and drinking, along with whatever sexual life-style one chooses. It is very easy for counselling services to buy into this 'feel good' model.

The whole of this book has attempted to explore notions of ecclesial community from a holistic valuing of creation. It goes without saying that this includes embodied expressions of our being-in-relation like the sharing of meals and the joy of sexual relationships. To worship the God of the garden is, among other things, to savour the delights of sensuous pleasure. It is not to run away from the rediscovery and revaluing of *eros*, since to follow Jesus is to remember a man who 'came eating and drinking'. But the authentic richness of the spiritualities of Christian tradition is *counter-cultural* in challenging the particular excesses and distorted moralities of the day. Whether we speak of the radical witness of the early Christian martyrs, the eschatological sharpness of the challenge of the first monks in the desert, Francis of Assisi's witness to radical poverty, or the non-violent witness of the contemporary peace movement, the spirituality which burgeons at a specific time offers an authentic counter-cultural witness as a concrete embodiment of Jesus' vision of the kindom of right relations. *The authentic ecclesial spirituality for which I search should not be that of helping us to fit comfortably into the status quo.* 'Transforming' as a dimension of *ecclesia* (Chapter 7) seeks to be resourced by the tools, ingredients and practices of a spirituality which counters the myopic indulgence of the age through imagining, enabling and embodying meaningful alternatives.

The second problem is that the word itself carries negative overtones of spiritual dualisms. It is undeniable that there are ongoing tensions between body, mind, soul and spirit. It is part of the human condition that it seems hard to get up in the morning when the body cries out for more sleep, just as it is far from easy to control appetites for eating and drinking. That is not the issue. The problem comes – as feminist philosophers and theologians have tirelessly pointed out – that in the interpretation and living out of these contrasts, so often the physical side of the body/mind contrast is devalued, and this devalued physicality is associated with women. In traditional interpretations – which linger on in our psyches and unconscious attitudes – women have come to represent human nature in its less noble aspect. Thus body/nature/feeling/ earth/women/animals have come to be classed as inferior (= immanent), over against mind/spirit/soul/men (= transcendent). Men were then viewed (for example by Augustine) as more capable of embodying the God-image.[4]

A counter-cultural spirituality has to go further than merely analysing this tension: it has to enable a way forward, valuing the body, sexuality and the materiality of the whole of existence. But it must do this without either falling into the self-indulgence of the 'salvation-in-the-sauna' mentality, or eliminating the possibility of the renunciation of bodily comforts and active sexual relationships, where *this is freely undertaken in the name of the authentic ecclesial struggle for transformation.*

The third difficulty is that spirituality must be in some way grounded in a theology of the Holy Spirit. Yet the Western tradition has – up till the recent renewal – been deficient in attention and understanding of the Spirit. Indeed, one writer observed that whenever 'most of us say God, the Holy Spirit never comes immediately to mind; rather, the Spirit seems like an edifying appendage to the doctrine of God'.[5] In an extremely popular radio programme, *Priestland's Progress*, the late Gerald Priestland referred to the Holy Spirit as 'the guest who came to dinner and stayed on to become a member of the family'![6] Words have been used to describe the Holy Spirit such as 'vague', 'shadowy', 'faceless', 'homeless in the west' (Ratzinger), 'the half-known God' (Congar), and the Cinderella of theology.[7] It almost seems to continue the process of devaluing the Spirit to concede that 'he' might be the 'feminine' dimension of the Godhead (which is the approach of Leonardo Boff).[8]

There is an additional problem when approaching the mystery of Spirit from a theology of Church. For the Church often gives the impression of controlling and organizing the dispensing of the Spirit in a way which seems opposed to the radical freedom 'which blows where it will' (John 3:8). It is this radical freedom of the holy *Ruah*,[9] a freedom promised for her children, which must be reclaimed for the dynamic movements of Church which I have been exploring.

In *The Wisdom of Fools?* I described the Spirit as the energy of connection, the life-energy of the cosmos, the energy of communion, the birth-giving energy which cracks open the false discourses of power and hypocrisy and allows the unheard, un-articulated stories to be heard.[10] Here the point to stress is that ushering in the millennium is a powerful epiphany of the Holy Spirit for our times. It is an epiphany which calls us both backwards and forwards. Backwards, to recover from the traditioning movement the experience that *spirituality is properly an ecclesial charism*, a way of being Church, but that like mysticism, it has been individualized and privatized. Forwards, to discover what the prophetic charism actually means today for becoming *ecclesia*. So the next step is to reclaim spiritual experience as being at the heart of Christian community, as well as being at the heart of living life to the full.

To be human is to have a spirituality ... but what kind?

> The Christian of the future will be a mystic or he or she will not exist at all. If by mysticism we mean, not singular parapsychological phenomena, but a genuine experience of God emerging from the heart of our existence, this statement is very true and its truth and importance will become clearer in the spirituality of the future ... Possession of the Spirit is not something of which we are made factually aware merely by pedagogic indoctrination as a reality beyond our existential awareness, but is experienced inwardly. (Karl Rahner[11])

These words point to the heart of Karl Rahner's conviction: to be fully human is to be oriented to the mystery of transcendent being. It is to be reaching out beyond the limits of human frailty, to be radically questioning, ceaselessly searching, but always from the specific context of ordinary living. The quest for the transcendent in no way removes humanity from this sphere; indeed, Rahner tries to deepen the connection between spirituality and everyday life. He is well aware that the 'spiritual professionals' of the monasteries would formally strive for perfection, freed from the myriads of distractions of, for example, the need to earn the daily bread, the misery of unemployment, the desperate lack of sleep of the young mother or the round-the-clock needs of the Alzheimer's sufferer. Even if we do not agree with all his ideas, for example, that of 'anonymous Christians',[12] for contemporary spirituality he has blazed a trail for rooting *mysticism* in the life of the ordinary Christian, as well as locating spirituality at the heart of the journey of every human being, religious and secular alike. As he wrote: 'The root of all spirituality lies in the act of entrusting the plurality of one's life calmly and silently to God.'[13] The Dutch theologian Otto Steggink similarly describes spirituality as

> expressing in behaviour the deepest motivation from which you live, your

lifestyle, the way you see, feel and act on personal, interpersonal and societal levels. Spirituality . . . is thus a dynamic process . . . and as such has to do with growth and learning processes, with stages and crises of development, with formation, guidance and discernment of spirits.[14]

But Rahner also wanted to point the way to a 'communal experience of the Spirit'.[15] At a time when this communal experience is popularly seen in terms of the rather sensational charismatic gifts of speaking in tongues, healing and prophecy, not to mention the Toronto Blessing, Rahner's intuition recalls us not only to the ancient theological and liturgical traditions of the Orthodox Church, where the spiritual experience of the whole community is at the heart of the Liturgy, but to the New Testament theology of Paul, for whom the community was the crucial sacred space for remembering and handing on what had happened in the Cross and Resurrection events (1 Corinthians 15:3). Whatever happened in the fledgling churches, conflicts of ethics and theological truth alike were always referred back to the flourishing of the community. It is exactly this communal witness – not merely the holiness of exceptional individuals – which is now at stake. And it is no accident that, in an individualistic society it is precisely this which eludes us. *But if we could bring it back, if we could embody again the prophetic, mystical community, would we see the dawn breaking on our Dark Night?*

If to be human is to have a spirituality, and if to be *ecclesia* is to be empowered and animated communally by the Spirit of God, what are the essential currents of contemporary spirituality which will lead us forward? That spirituality is always influenced by its context is no surprise. I have warned that much of what passes for spirituality today is influenced by excessive individualism and a dearth of relational sensitivity. At the other end of the spectrum, Otto Steggink has warned that if spirituality becomes too identified with the public arena, it is 'often nothing else than a whole package of civil values and norms, given a Christian and religious wrapping'.[16]

As a means of discerning the way forward, I look to the *transforming dimension* of being Church as crucial. So it is Christ, as transformer of culture who blazes the trail forward.[17] I look to the currents of spirituality which confront the individualism, the violent and death-dealing dimensions of culture with life-giving alternatives. So I look to creation spirituality, spiritualities of justice and a spirituality of mystical contemplation, viewed from an ecclesial focus as well as from the perspective of the individual's journey.

There can be no hesitation about putting a spirituality for political and social justice for poor communities on a global scale at the centre of the concerns of contemporary spirituality. If spirituality is to be understood not as a luxury for the well-off who seek a way to cope with the stress of life, but as the enabling of the well-being of the whole 'discipleship of equals',[18] then the conditions, the context and survival and the *flourishing* of the poor communities of Africa, Asia, Latin America, and their counterparts in the northern hemisphere are our principal aim as we approach the millennium with the task of 'gathering the fragments'. As the Columban priest Ed O'Connell put it in an article which sets the scriptural call for Jubilee at the centre of the preparation for the millennium, linking the themes of transforming and dreaming:

> While we walk with this experience and this hope, we are called to provoke temporary and partial jubilees, 'moments of justice', here and there, in the Church and in society. Even if the world is resistant, and the Church frequently opaque, we must not let the dream go stale. Because when we dream, it is God who dreams in us. Our mission is to inaugurate new ways, new experiments, new signs of the coming Kingdom. And we are called to start with ourselves and with the Church, adventuring in new styles of life, new gestures.[19]

From the poorest communities, marked by suffering and resistance, come the most evocative glimpses of the longed-for alternatives. Here faith, prayer and communal action for justice unite to form a seamless whole. As Leonardo Boff wrote, in the very struggle for justice, new kinds of asceticism arise:

> Here, more real and different virtues emerge: solidarity with one's class, participation in community decisions, loyalty to the decisions that are defined, the overcoming of hatred against those who are agents of the mechanisms of impoverishment, the capacity to see beyond the immediate present, and to work for a society which is not yet visible and will never be enjoyed. This new type of asceticism . . . has demands and renunciations of its own.[20]

The women theologians' dialogue in Costa Rica (1994),[21] with sharp awareness and deep concern at the rising tide of violence against women, articulated the interrelation of risk, hope and struggle as elements both of spirituality and conditions for survival itself.[22] Chung Hyun Kyung's anguished story of the 'comfort woman', Soo Bock, who survived the violent abuse of the Japanese soldiers through a 'spirituality for life', evokes the question as to who or what is the source of a decision to eat, to hang on in hope. It is the mystery behind those who survived the Holocaust, the source of the strength of Etty Hillesum (Chapter 2), the mothers of the 'Disappeared' in Argentina, the courage of Rigoberta Menchú from Guatemala. As Denise Ackermann mused:

> Soo-Bock's 'spirituality for life' in the face of overwhelming odds flowers again at the age of seventy-four. Was the foundation for this spirituality laid long ago when she risked running away from her leprous husband, when she decided to

eat in order to survive, and when she married, despite past experiences? I do not know. Could it be that the mysterious alchemy of risk, hope and struggle was at work in this woman's life? And the question remains: What is the source of this mysterious alchemy? In reflecting on Hyun Kyung's list of divine powers, such as Ki, Chi, Shakti, Prana, ruah, and so on, I am thrown back on my faith concepts. I have a hunch and more than a hunch, that God is the breath inside the breath, the source of all that is life-giving.[23]

The challenge then is for the Church — in all the dimensions of journeying, dwelling, traditioning, transforming and dreaming — to relinquish the idea that she *dispenses and controls* the Holy *Ruah* of God; equally she needs to lose the fear that the Spirit is experienced outside of official structures. If the Spirit indeed blows where she will, it would be strange for her not to be found wherever there is struggle for justice and the flourishing of the well-being of the entire creation.

Through commitment to struggle for justice the prophetic charism of *ecclesia* is revivified.[24] The tension between the prophetic dimension and institution of the Church is so deeply felt that it actually constitutes part of the impasse of the Dark Night. As I have been arguing throughout the book, the object is to understand the *necessary form* of good governance, structures and practices to bring the churches out of the Dark Night: to reject government in favour of anarchic enthusiasm, a woolly commitment to majority consensus, or a nostalgic attempt to return to the ragged bands on the shores of Galilee is sheer folly. This is not *dreaming ecclesia* but misguided infantilism. The resolution of the impasse will be facilitated if we can find a way to honour, not the individual, but the prophetic community.[25]

In the context of a spirituality of justice on the threshold of the millennium, attention to context is the first step. The prophetic action required by the North differs from that of the South. We in the North can practise effective solidarity, can listen, learn, develop a compassionate praxis, but it is first and foremost the task of the poor communities themselves to articulate their priorities. As I write, the news has just come through that Rodolfo Cardenal, whose views on 'the crucified peoples' are referred to in Chapter 1, has been 'relieved' of his parish work in San Salvador, as part of action against the Jesuits of the University of Central America.[26] Again, an example of the failure to listen to the cry of the people themselves. Again a tragic blindness to the way that the Jesuits — six of whom were murdered — are blazing a prophetic trail in terms of bringing back theological education to its roots in justice for poor people.

Here in the North, the priority is to become prophetic communities whose life-style makes it possible for poor communities of the South to survive, to live, and live with all the necessities of human dignity. As an *ecclesia* which truly *dwells* in a specific bio-region, these communities will refuse to give way to consumerism: they cry 'Enough!' They will fight the over-consumption which has created insatiable demands for exotic, out-of-season foods, drink and drugs, clothes, cars and every form of manufactured gadget. But to do this means recovering *eucharistic* communities where the sacrifice we offer embraces a culture of sacrifice, restraint and simplicity which touches every form of our lives. Here we can recover the balance between honouring creation – as Annie Dillard was sent into ecstasy with the 'tree of lights' (Chapter 8) – reverencing the limits of its resources, and fashioning a *eucharistic praxis* together. This is a far cry from the traditional notion of sacrifice, which, in the past, has seemed to glorify suffering, condoning violence and accepting the scapegoat syndrome, with all the tragic consequences for women and marginalized groups.

Secondly, prophetic communities attempt to live in a way which condemns this culture of violence – this *necrophilic* or *death-dealing* culture – and lives in a way which opens pathways to life-giving, life-enhancing possibilities, where glimpses of light warm the frozen, fragmented contexts. This is a fraught path: where the political response to what is seen as the collapse of 'moral fibre' is to impose – once more – order from above, with political parties competing for the moral high ground, over-simplified solutions renege on the richer possibilities of this *kairos* moment. It is myopic to call for the restoration of 'the family' without admitting that the family structure has frequently allowed violent situations to continue, even to the point of death – usually of women and children but occasionally of men. It is myopic because the nuclear family of the North and West is far from the structure of the household/*oikos* which was, for a time, the means of the growth of the New Testament Church. Stability and order will never be achieved by suppression of the truth. The concept of *ecclesia* I have been hoping for, Church as enabler of many communities, means that prophetic Church will actively enable all groups who tackle the roots of violence in small children, groups who organize refuges for abused women, groups – like Church Action for Poverty – who stress the links between poverty, homelessness and a breakdown of stable family relationships. Tolerance of irregularity rather than insistence on conformity to rules, widening the parameters of eucharistic community as a way forward from social fragmentation, discerning the goodness in relationships which fail to conform to the norm and enabling the financial means for these fragile unions to flourish – is this not the only way forward for creatively engaging the chaos and for prophetic boundary living?

Above all, communities of prophecy will be safe spaces of trusting where women can speak the truth of their abuse, suffering and rejection, without fear. The numerous witnesses to the difficulties of speaking out, through fear of criticism, disbelief or downright rejection are now overwhelming.[27] This means a further dimension to eucharistic community: it means rethinking the relationship between justice, forgiveness and reconciliation. If the priority is healing for the victim of violence, there has to be a far deeper understanding of the processes that leads to forgiveness and reconciliation. Too often the simplistic repetition of the adage 'forgive and forget', coupled with Jesus' injunction to forgive seventy times over, ignores the wider scriptural context where forgiveness is linked with total conversion:

> Repent and turn from all your transgressions . . . and get yourselves a new heart and a new spirit . . . so turn, and live! (Ezekiel 18.30–32)

But this focus on the offender depends on him or her being willing to repent. Most often, we are dealing with situations where the offender is definitely not willing to repent: the community has to put compassion into action by helping the victim out of a state of total devastation, a sense of shame and worthlessness. Marie Fortune outlines a method which includes truth-telling and acknowledgement of the harm done to the victim.[28] The method also involves breaking the silence which surrounds the whole issue of violence, refusing to minimize its significance, and protecting the vulnerable child or woman from further abuse. One of the ways we see the activity of the Holy *Ruah* today is in the forms of mediation – be this in contexts of marriage breakdown, in the more agonizing forms of abuse, or in the complexity of work for peace: these are the most crucially important ways in which an entire community embodies the precious ministry of reconciliation:

> All this is from God, who through Christ reconciled us to himself and gave us the ministry of reconciliation: that is, in Christ God was reconciling the world to himself, not counting their trespasses against them, and entrusting to us the message of reconciliation. (2 Corinthians 5:18–19)

By emphasizing the communal dimension of the spiritual practices of reconciliation, the weight is lifted from this being regarded as a personal failure if a woman cannot forgive.[29] For we are acknowledging that the roots of violence sink deep into complex structures of emotional deprivation, ignorance, poverty, a tolerated level of misogyny, a fear of rocking the boat of what is imagined to be the stability of marriage and a loss of a sense of belonging to a responsible moral community.

The very gravity of this situation leads to the second characteristic of a spirituality for the Dark Night – that of *mystical contemplation viewed as a community way of life.* This is not to spurn the witness of an individual's visionary life, or to acknowledge that this is happening today in all kinds of contexts, but to maintain that such is the gravity of our situation that only a mystical faith will save us now. The resources of the mystical traditions are indeed precious – but could there be a new way of mystical contemplation appropriate for this context, and practised in community? Dorothee Soelle speaks of mysticism and resistance as the way forward:

> The language of religion, by which I do not mean the stolen language in which a male God commands and radiates imperial power, the language of religion is the language of mysticism: I am entirely and wholly in God, I cannot fall out of God at all, I am indestructible.[30]

But this God in whom I live, move and have my being is so far away from the transcendent male God of Power and might that I struggle for words and images to keep alive a faith for the Dark Night. Those who know this reality know it, not as a place of creativity, or of being powerfully energized by new currents of thought, experience or exciting relationships. It is a place of lostness, often scandalous confusion and a sense of abandonment.[31] There is a dearth of nurture and a eucharistic famine – from the very sources from which they could expect nourishment. But if there is to be a new birth of *ecclesia*, it will only come through practising contemplation in this Dark Night. When we have no clear-cut solutions, that is when a solidarity of compassion with suffering people and suffering earth, and the practice of endurance and sustaining brokenness – including our own – are the only ways forward. There is aloneness – but there is connection in this aloneness, since the authentic isolation of the contemplative creates the very means of deeper solidarity and ability to sustain the suffering of isolation and opposition. It can be no accident that in this world where so much of what is named community is a mere parody of it, where intimacy and communion are most deeply yearned for and most frequently absent, the revelation given to us is that solitude and communion are two sides of the same coin. The late May Sarton tumbled to this discovery in a year recorded in *Journal of a Solitude*;[32] here she cites Louis Lavelle, *Le Mal et Le Souffrance*:

> We sense that there can be no true communion between human beings, until they have in fact become human beings: for to be able to give oneself one must have taken possession of oneself in that painful solitude outside of which nothing belongs to us and we have nothing to give ... [33]

And, more crucially, we need the ability to sustain what is frequently not seen as vision, but a conviction that there is a deeper truth, an integrity to which we must give witness, or our lives are worthless.

In all of this, God remains God, but God has made God's very self vulnerable to our response. Incarnation is not merely 'the hint, half-guessed' (T. S. Eliot), but the very pattern, the leitmotiv of divine vulnerability. Annie Dillard has expressed it movingly:

> There is no one but us. There is no one to send, nor a clean hand, nor a pure heart on the face of the earth, nor in the earth, but only us, a generation comforting ourselves with the notion that we have come at an awkward time, that our innocent fathers are all dead – as if innocence had ever been – and our children busy and troubled, and we ourselves unfit, not yet ready ... and grown exhausted, unable to seek the thread, weak and involved. But there is no one but us. There never has been.[34]

There is no one but us – but we are not alone. For God not only reveals presence-in-vulnerability but also presence-in-wisdom, *Sophia, Hokmah*. What will lead us out of darkness is the recovery of this vulnerability in the cosmic suffering of God, in the wonderment at cosmic processes which we have gradually lost, in *earth wisdom as foundational for our eucharistic communities*. As Thomas Berry wrote, 'Where else can we go for the dream of the Earth'?[35] To recover and celebrate eucharistically the vibrant yet vulnerable presence of the epiphanic God as the revivifying power of the suffering and groaning earth, vulnerable to our thunderous tread and inexhaustible consumption, that is surely the way out of the Dark Night of the Church, the recovery of soul and the mending of our fragmentation ...

> Help us to be the always hopeful
> Gardeners of the Spirit
> Who know that without darkness
> nothing comes to birth
> As without light
> Nothing flowers.[36]

Notes

1 Chung Hyun Kyung's address to the World Council of Churches' Assembly in Canberra (Australia), 1991, cited in Sallie McFague, 'Holy Spirit' in *Dictionary of Feminist Theologies*, ed. Letty Russell and Shannon Clarkson (Louisville, KY: Westminster John Knox, 1996), p. 147.

2 Joann Wolski Conn, 'Toward spiritual maturity' in *Freeing Theology: The Essentials of Theology in Feminist Perspective*, ed. Catherine Mowry LaCugna (HarperSanFrancisco, 1993), pp. 235–59.

3 'Spiritual' has carried a variety of meanings throughout history. 'Spirituality' in the seventeenth century meant the 'interior life of Christians'. 'Devotion' or 'piety' were more

frequently used words, where the reference was often to a set of practices. The publication of the *Dictionnaire de la Spiritualité* (Paris, 1960) has been influential in the word 'spirituality' assuming the meaning of 'the whole realm of experience and practices involving the human spirit and the soul dimension of existence': Conn, 'Toward spiritual maturity', p. 236.

4 See Val Plumwood, *Feminism and the Mastery of Nature* (London: Routledge, 1993). The Augustine text referred to is *De Trinitate* 7.7, 10.

5 Heribert Mühlen, 'The person of the Holy Spirit' in *The Holy Spirit and Power*, ed. Kilian McDonnell (Garden City, NY: Doubleday, 1975), p. 12.

6 Gerald Priestland, 'The guest who came to dinner' in *Priestland's Progress: One Man's Search for Christianity Now* (London: BBC Publications, 1981), pp. 106–19.

7 Cited in Elizabeth Johnson, *She Who Is* (New York: Crossroad, 1994), p. 130.

8 See L. Boff, *The Maternal Face of God* (London: Collins, 1989). For an acute critique of this approach see Sarah Coakley, 'Mariology and "romantic feminism": a critique' in *Women's Voices: Essays in Contemporary Feminist Theology*, ed. Teresa Elwes (London: Marshall Pickering, 1992). pp. 99–110.

9 I use the Hebrew work *Ruah* as seeming to encapsulate the raw, elemental power of the Spirit, characteristic of her activity in the Bible.

10 *The Wisdom of Fools?* (London: SCM, 1993), pp. 128–33.

11 Karl Rahner, 'The spirituality of the Church of the future' in *Theological Investigations*, vol. 20, tr. Edward Quinn (London: Darton, Longman and Todd, 1981), p. 149; cited in Declan Marmion, 'The notion of spirituality in Karl Rahner', *Louvain Studies* 26.1 (1996), pp. 61–86.

12 The idea that in reaching out to the transcendent, rooted in whatever context or faith community, one is always fundamentally Christian, or pseudo-Christian relating to the Christ mystery, is not acceptable to other faith communities and is a false starting-point for genuine interfaith dialogue.

13 Marmion, 'The notion of spirituality in Karl Rahner', p. 86.

14 Otto Steggink, 'Spiritualiteit, Wat is dat eigenlijk?', *Verbum Dei* 47.4 (1980), p. 237. (My translation from Dutch.)

15 Rahner, 'The spirituality of the Church of the future', p. 151.

16 Otto Steggink, 'Spiritualiteit was nooit zonder Tijdgeest', *Speling* 37.1 (1985), p. 20. (My translation.)

17 As is obvious, I am referring to H. R. Niebuhr, *Christ and Culture* (New York, 1951), where he sketched the different possible relations between Christianity and culture as being (1) Christ against culture, (2) Christ of culture, (3) Christ above culture, (4) Christ and culture in paradox, and (5) Christ, the transformer of culture.

18 The phrase is Elisabeth Schüssler Fiorenza's: *In Memory of Her* (London: SCM, 1983), pp. 140ff.

19 Ed O'Connell, 'Towards a just millennium' in *The Millennium Jubilee*, ed. Brian Davies, Mary Grey et al. (London: CAFOD, 1996), p. 35.

20 Leonardo Boff, 'The need for political saints: from a spirituality of liberation to the practice of liberation', *Crosscurrents* XXX.4 (1981), p. 375.

21 See M. Mananzan, M. Oduyoye, E. Tamez, S. Clarkson, M. Grey and L. Russell (eds), *Women Resisting Violence: A Spirituality for Life* (Maryknoll: Orbis, 1996).

22 See the contribution of Denise Ackermann, 'The alchemy of risk, struggle and hope', ibid., pp. 141–6.

23 Ackermann, ibid., p. 146.

24 I develop the prophetic and mystical charisms of *ecclesia* in the Scottish Journal of Theology Lectures (December 1996): to be published as *Prophecy and Mysticism: The Heart of the Postmodern Church* (Edinburgh: T. & T. Clark, 1997).

25 I do not suggest that this is the only way, or one which solves the thorny issues of ordained ministry and apostolic succession. But a different focus will offer a new way forward.

26 As reported in *The Tablet* (26 October 1996).

27 See Carol J. Adams and Marie M. Fortune (eds), *Violence Against Women and Children: A Christian Theological Coursebook* (New York: Continuum, 1995). For a particularly horrifying story of incest and a failure to reach justice in Church contexts, see Linda H. Hollies, 'When the mountain won't move', ibid., pp. 314–27.

28 Fortune, *Violence against Women*, p. 203.

29 'A group of incest offenders in a treatment program made a powerful plea: "Don't forgive so easily". All were Christians and had gone to their pastors as soon as they were arrested, asking to be forgiven. Each had been prayed over, forgiven, and sent home. They said that this pastoral response had been least helpful to them because it enabled them to continue to avoid accountability for their offenses': Fortune, ibid., pp. 205–6.

30 Dorothee Soelle, 'Liberating our God-talk: from authoritarian otherness to mystical inwardness' in *Liberating Women: New Theological Dimensions* (European Society of Women in Theological Research, University of Bristol, 1991), pp. 40–52 (quotation p. 45).

31 I began to work on these ideas in *Redeeming the Dream* (London: SPCK, 1989), pp. 74–80.

32 May Sarton, *Journal of a Solitude* (New York: W. W. Norton, 1973; London: The Women's Press, 1985).

33 Ibid., p. 89.

34 Annie Dillard, *Holy the Firm*, cited in Anne Kelly editorial, 'Imagining peace', *The Shanty Times* (Spring 1996).

35 Thomas Berry, *The Dream of the Earth*, p. 223.

36 May Sarton, 'Kali' from *A Grain of Mustard Seed*; cited in *Journal of a Solitude*, p. 56.

INDEX